THE RENTER'S RIGHTS HANDBOOK

by Robert Shemin

To Kathy,
Nice meeting you,
Thanks,

Bryan
1997

Publicity by Jim Floyd/Jimmy Hank Promotions
          1150 Troxel Road
          Lansdale, PA 19446
          215-855-3192

Homepage: WWW.Rent588.edge.net

Editor: Susan Blankenship/Digital Dog Design, Nashville

Cover Design: Larry Blankenship/Digital Dog Design, Nashville

Published by: Big Boy Publishing
               P.O. Box 128186
               Nashville, TN 37212-8186
               Facsimile: 615-383-9911

Write to the author at the above address

DISCLAIMER: This book is intended for general information only. Laws often change, so please consult a local attorney before acting upon any of the information contained in this book.

Acknowledgment

To my lovely wife Patricia and to the best big boy in the world, Alexander, my son — thank you for your love and patience while writing all of this.

A special thank you to Larry and Susan Blankenship of Digital Dog Design and funhouse. Thank you to the fine ladies at Dowling Press, Maryglenn McCombs and Susan Sachs. Not much would be possible without Susan Garrabrant.

Also, my appreciation to all of my renters, who constantly teach me things everyday. To Mark Feemston and First Union Bank, thank you for the capital and the good times. How about the best manager in the world — Jim Floyd of Jimmy Hank Promotions. Let the festivities begin...

Contents

THE RENTER'S RIGHTS HANDBOOK

MISSION:

Renters should be treated like valued customers. The landlord-renter relationship should be a positive and productive one with everyone understanding and respecting each other's rights and responsibilities.

Introduction

Why You Should Read This Book

If you are about to rent your first house or apartment, this book will explain the entire process to you and save you a lot of headaches and hopefully hundreds of dollars.

If you are thinking about moving you will know how to get your deposit back, get a good reference, and how to find a good place with a great landlord.

If you are having problems with your current landlord you will learn your rights as a renter and how to better negotiate with your landlord..

You will learn how to interview a landlord.

You will learn how to train your landlord.

Learn the money saving secret about discounted rent.

What to do if you cannot pay this month's rent.

1

Getting Started

Finding a place to live

There are so many ways to begin looking for a new place to live. This section will teach you the common ways to find a good place to live, but will also show you many more creative ways to find a place. Most people look for a new place to live backwards. Whether they are renting or buying a home, most people look for the place first, inspect it second, fill out an application or loan request third, and then finally determine whether they can afford it or not. Let me save you a lot of aggravation. First, determine the rent or payment you can afford, then begin to look.

Example: You do not usually go to the mall, pick out the nicest piece of jewelry or clothing you can find, walk to the checkout and then realize you cannot afford it. What you should do is set some kind of budget and then begin to shop. The same is true for finding a place to live. Set your budget first, and then

1

begin to look in your price range. By the way, just to make you feel a little better, studies show that everyone, from the person with the lowest income to the multi-millionaire, wants to live in a nicer place that they cannot afford! You are not alone.

How Much Rent Can You Afford?

My Budget

Name:
Date:
Address:
Social Security Number:
Employer:

Income

Net Monthly Income	A	_____
Other Income (specify sources)	B	_____
Total Net Monthly Income (A + B)	C	_____

Fixed Expenses

Monthly Car Payments	D	_____
Monthly furniture payments/rental	E	_____
Insurance	F	_____
Education/Tuition	G	_____
Credit Card Payments (monthly avg.)	H	_____
Other Fixed Monthly Payments (specify: child support, alimony, etc.)	I	_____
Total Fixed Expenses (add D through I)	**J**	_____

Variable Monthly Expenses (please use averages)

Food	K	_____
Utilities	L	_____
Clothing	M	_____
Entertainment	N	_____
Travel	O	_____

Other Bills (please specify)	P	_____
Total Variable Monthly		*Expenses*
(add K through P)	Q	_____

Net/Net Monthly Income
(amount available to pay rent)

Total Monthly Income	C	_____
- Fixed Monthly Income -	J	_____
- Variable Monthly Income -	Q	_____
= *Net/Net Monthly Income* =	R	_____

The budget you just prepared will let you know how much you have available every month to pay the rent.

Rent Rules

Some general rules about how much rent you can afford are:

1. 25% of your gross monthly pay
> **Example:** You earn $1,800 per month
> x 0.25
> $450.00 per month

Many of us pay 30% or 40% of our gross monthly pay in rent. This is unfortunate as it does not leave much for utilities, food, transportation, etc. Many people even pay 50% of their gross monthly income in rent. Please be very careful.

2. One week's gross pay. This is the same as 25% of your gross income.

3. 70% of your net/net take home money as prepared in your budget above. This leaves 30% of your money for savings and emergencies.

Of course, you do have some control over the money you earn and spend, so if you are not happy with the amount you currently have available for your monthly rent, consider some of the following options:

1. Increase your income
- get a better job
- obtain more training to get a raise
- take on a second job

Or:

2. Cut your expenses
- review your budget and find areas where you can save money
- use coupons and buy items on sale
- buy less
- sell some of your belongings
- change your lifestyle to a less expensive one.

What do I Really Want to Rent?

Once you have determined how much rent you can comfortably and realistically afford, you should begin your search. Just as important as knowing how much you can pay in rent, is knowing what kind of place you want to rent. The following questions may help you determine exactly what you are looking for. So many renters just jump at the first place they find only to discover later, usually within 10 days of emptying the last moving box, that they are miserable. Take your time and answer these questions in writing:

1. I want to live in the following areas:
First Choice: _____
Second Choice: _____
Third Choice: _____

2. I want to live in (check whichever apply):
an apartment in a small building   _____

an apartment in a large building   _____
a condo   _____
a duplex   _____
a triplex   _____
a house   _____
a new building   _____
an old building   _____

3. The following amenities are important to me:

exercise room   _____
clubhouse   _____
pool   _____
tennis court   _____
doorman   _____
laundry room   _____
other (specify)   _____

4. I need the following in my apartment or house:

refrigerator   _____
stove   _____
microwave oven   _____
central air conditioning   _____
window unit air conditioning   _____
ceiling fans   _____
central heat   _____
heating units   _____
washer/dryer hookups   _____
other (specify)   _____

5. I want to park my car:

on the street   _____
in a covered parking lot   _____
in a marked parking spot   _____
in a garage   _____
in a carport   _____

6. I want to live within walking distance of:

bus   _____

train   _____

subway   _____

grocery store   _____

shopping   _____

entertainment   _____

7. I want the following security features:

security guard   _____

doorman   _____

security gate   _____

alarm   _____

other (specify)   _____

8. I want ____ bedrooms

9. I want ____ bathrooms

10. I want to live on:

one level   _____

two levels   _____

more than two levels   _____

11. The place needs to have:

an elevator   _____

handicapped access   _____

12. I want to live around:

single people   _____

couples   _____

children   _____

older residents   _____

13. I want the community to be:

noisy   _____

quiet   _____

lively, with a lot of resident parties_____

14. The management should be:
on site   _____
off site   _____

Making these decisions now will help you determine what you are looking for. They are meant just as guides so that you can begin your search as an informed renter. Decide what you can afford and what you want, and you increase your chances of finding it.

Choosing the Right Area or Neighborhood

Many people know exactly where in a town or region they would like to live. However, most Americans now move every three years or so on average, which means that many of us will be faced at some time with moving to a city or area we do not know well at all. If you are new to your city or town and are not sure which area is best for you, you will want to make sure that you choose a neighborhood that suits your needs and is safe for you and your family. The following are some ideas that may help you determine what part of town you want to be in. Many of these recommendations also apply to an apartment building or area once you have narrowed your search.

1. Ask the following people for ideas and recommendations:
- friends
- relatives
- employers
- the Chamber of Commerce
- co-workers
- a realtor
- apartment locator services

2. Check on the crime rate. The best thing to do if you want to find out about the safety of a particular area is to call the police department. They should be ready, willing, and able to help. Talk to officers who actually patrol the area. They will be best qualified to tell you what it is like.

3. Drive or walk through the Area. Check out the area yourself by day and at night to see if you feel comfortable there. If you really want to know what an area is like, drive by late on a Friday or Saturday night. Many neighborhoods that look fine during the day can turn into wild party areas after dark on weekends.

4. Look At the Cars Parked in the Streets. You can tell a lot by the type of cars parked in an area. Notice if they are newer and nicer, or older and junkier. Ask yourself what kind of people probably drive these cars and if you will feel comfortable living near them.

5. Talk to Neighbors. Talking to people who live there can give you a good idea of what the area is like and whether you want to move there.

Finding a New Place

Consult section 2, ***Rent for Little, Rent for Less, Rent for Free***, before you commit to a new place, as many of the ideas given there could help you in your search. Some of the most common ways to find a new place to live are:

1. Looking in the newspaper in the For Rent section.

2. Getting a local apartment guide book (available in most cities at newspaper stands, grocery stores, etc.)

3. Using an apartment referral service.

4. Driving and looking for "For Rent" signs.

5. Asking your friends, acquaintances, co-workers, employers, and religious leaders for referrals.

6. Check smaller local newspapers too. They often have really good deals on rental property.

7. Look under "Property Management" in the Yellow Pages. These are firms that manage properties and they may have a place for you. Whomever you speak to, you should ask for referrals. If you call on an ad or sign and the people you speak to do not know of a place for you, ask them if they could recommend a company or person who might have a place available. If a property manager has a free moment, you may want to have them tell you about the areas of town in which you are interested.

8. Run an ad in the newspaper advertising the fact that you are looking for a place or a particular type of living situation.

> **Example:** Responsible couple seeks to rent two-bedroom house with yard for about $495/month in _____ (specify areas of town). Call xxx-xxxx (your number).

9. Check university bulletin boards. At certain times of the year, especially during the summer, they may list many available places.

10. Contact your church, synagogue or religious organization and read their newsletters.

11. If you are a member of a professional association, civic group or club, you may want to **get the word out that you are looking for a place.** Put a short article in the newsletter, use flyers, or simply tell as many members as you can and ask them to spread the word that you are looking for a place.

When Should You Begin to Look for a New Place to Live?

When you should begin to look depends on your market. For instance, in some cities where it is very difficult to find a place to live, you should give yourself as much time as possible to look. However, many landlords will not hold a place for more than 30-45 days. For this reason, try to start your search about 60 days before you need to move.

This will give you plenty of time to locate a nice place and perhaps you can apply to be approved and hold it for about 30 days, giving you plenty of time to organize your move. Remember that demand differs greatly from area to area; you may have to begin your search many months before you move.

When you begin to call on places and talk to landlords and property managers in your area, ask them:

1.How far in advance of moving they recommend you start to look.

2. How long they can hold a place for you once your application has been approved.

Questions and Answers for Renters Getting Started

Q. What should I look for when I am trying to find a new place to rent?

A. Check out the following:

1. Budget. You should make out a budget (See page 2.) so that you can see what you can afford. Do not shop for a new place backwards. Most people find what they want and then realize they cannot afford it. You should shop the right way. Be sure of what you can afford, and then begin to look for a place that is within your budget.

2. Availability. You should find out what is available in your price range. Look in the newspapers, all of the big ones and smaller neighborhood papers. Look for apartment locator guides, call the chamber of commerce. Get referrals from your employer, fellow employees, friends, relatives, and religious leaders as to what is available. Talk to property managers and real estate agents (you can find them in the Yellow Pages). Try contacting the housing offices of any nearby universities or visit them to see what is available.

3. Amenities. Make a list of what you want (See page 5.). Check for appliances, central heat and air, laundry facilities, pool, clubhouse, security, etc.

4. Location. Make sure the place you are looking at is near what you need. How far is it from work, public transportation, shopping, entertainment, etc?

5. Security. Safety is an issue now for everyone, everywhere. Find out about the area where you are thinking about living. Ask the landlord, ask the neighbors, and talk to the police about the safety of the area. Educate yourself as to lighting, parking, types of locks and other security measures that are available. Is there on-site security? A doorman? Cameras? Make sure there is at least one smoke detector on every floor of the rental unit.

Q. Are you allowed to see the specific unit that you are going to rent?

A: You absolutely should be allowed to, and should inspect the actual unit that you are going to rent. Often, landlords will tell you that "all of the places are the same" and will not show you the exact unit that you are going to rent. You must thoroughly inspect the unit before you agree to move in. Please fill out a move-in inspection sheet (see pages 51-54.) before you move into the new place.

This inspection is very, very important for two reasons:

1. It can help you to get your security deposit back. In order to get your security deposit back, you should be able to show that you are leaving the rental unit as you found it. Tenants are generally only responsible for damage beyond fair wear and tear. With a move-in inspection sheet, you can help protect your rights when the time comes for you to try to get your security deposit back.

2. It can help you avoid problems when you move. So many problems, headaches and ill will arise because a unit was not inspected thoroughly before someone moved in. So often, renters will rent a place without seeing it or inspecting it. Then, when they do move in, they become frustrated because something does not work, does not look like it should, the carpet is dirty or old, the shower does not work, or it is simply not what they expected. Inspect the unit and do not move into it until it is really ready. Save yourself a lot of hassles and perhaps a lot of money, too. If you move in without inspecting the property, you might have to move again and that could cost you big money. Inspect. Be happy!

2

Rent for Less, Rent for Little, Rent for Free

Save $1,000 this Year in Rent

Over 90% of renters pay the rent the landlord asks for. Please be in that elite 10% of renters who save hundreds if not thousands of dollars. Read on to find out many ways to save big dollars on your rent or even live for free. That's right! You *can* live rent free. Rest assured that renters all over the country are using these ideas to save money. You too could be one of them. Try some or all of these strategies for yourself. You may like them.

Rent for Less, Rent for Little
Negotiate

Rent is negotiable. Everyone always thinks that if the

13

landlord says the rent is $525 per month, then the price absolutely has to be $525 per month. The smart renter knows that this doesn't have to be true. If you never ask for or negotiate a lower rent, then you will never know if you could have received a better deal. Imagine how great it would be if, instead of paying the $525 per month your landlord asks for, you negotiate a rent of just $485 per month. You save:

> $40 this month
> or better yet
> $40 x 12 = $480 savings this year!

Think about it for a moment! $40 saved this month could be a very nice dinner for you and a friend or loved one. $480 could be a nice vacation for you this year. Wouldn't you prefer to keep that money in your own pocket rather than give it to your landlord?

Now, let's say that your rent is $895 per month. If you could negotiate it to $800 per month you save:

> $95 this month
> or
> $95 x 12 = $1140 this year!

These are real dollars, real savings, that could possibly be yours. How can you do it? **Just ask for a lower rent.** As the Bible says, "ask, and ye shall receive." If you never ask, you will never receive! When you ask, you might want to strengthen your case by pointing out what the rental unit lacks. For example, if the paint job is not perfect or the carpet needs cleaning, let the landlord know. You can also point out—and you must do this honestly—that:

> **a)** you really want the place, but cannot comfortably afford the rent and *"would you* (the landlord) *be nice*

enough to lower the rent?"

or better yet,

b) point out—and again, you must be truthful—that *"I* (the renter) *will take really great care of the place and will stay a long time."* Let the landlord know that you are a good tenant and will not bother the landlord and he or she may be more motivated to lower the rent.

Remember, most renters never ask. Don't make the same mistake! Ask. It could be worth hundreds, if not not thousands, of dollars to you.

Tips for Negotiating a Lower Rent

1. Listen. Find out what the landlord wants or needs.

2. Point out the benefits to the landlord. Explain to them why it will benefit them to give you what you want.

3. Say it Positively. People do not like to be challenged or threatened. ***Example:*** *"Give me lower rent or I will leave."* (This is your last resort!) ***Positively said, this would be:*** *"You would really be helping me out by lowering the rent and in the long run you will be better off, because you will have a good tenant, your place will not be empty, and I will take great care of it..."* Which do you think the landlord would rather hear?

4. He or She Who Speaks First Loses. When negotiating, if you say, *"I would like to rent this apartment, but I do not want to have to pay any more than $385 a month,"* don't say anything more. Whoever speaks first will lose. People do not like silence. So many of us get nervous and fill the silence with *"OK, OK, I can pay $410."* Let the landlord go first after you make an offer.

5. Let the landlord give you a larger discount. When negotiating your rent, try not to mention an exact amount. You may get a larger rent deduction than you anticipated.

> **Example:** If the landlord asks for $495, ask them what is the lowest amount of rent they could charge, understanding that you will be a great tenant. If you mention that you could pay $465, then the landlord might agree. If you do not mention an exact amount and let them speak, they may say $450. You could get an extra $15/month in savings, which you would not have received if you mentioned an exact amount.

6. Deal with Objections Quickly, or The Best Defense is an Offense. The landlord's objections are that they do not know you, they are not sure whether you will pay the rent and take care of the apartment or house. Deal with these objections up front, and quickly if you can. Show the landlord your good references and your credit report (see also *Putting in a better application*).

7. Be Flexible and Creative. Do not just ask for something one way. For example, if you want the rent lowered, but the landlord says no, ask again, but offer to pay the rent early or do some minor repair work.

8. Use Humor to Break the Tension. Be yourself, be relaxed and use some humor appropriately. Life is short: have a little fun! People who laugh together usually get along together.

9. Try Only to Negotiate with Decision Makers. Try to negotiate with the person who has the power to decide. You will be wasting your time and the other person's time if they are not the decision maker. If you ask someone for a lower rent and that person has to ask their manager then the communication may get garbled and confused. Very politely, try to ask if you can speak directly with the decision maker. Save yourself and everyone else some time.

Free Month of Rent or More

Some landlords offer a free month of rent to fill an empty apartment or house. Some landlords even offer 2 free months or 1½ months with the signing of a one or two year lease. If a free month is offered, ask for two months' free rent

Discounted Rent

You can really save $20-$100 a month! Remember, $35/month saved = $420/year. You can probably think of plenty of things to do with that money!

Discounted rent can work for you. Here's how. Normally, rent is due on the first of the month, but can sometimes be paid on the 5th or the 10th of the month without having to pay a late fee.

Important: Please review your lease or rental agreement to see exactly when your rent is due and when it is late.

When you are negotiating your rent before you move in to a new place, or when you are renewing your lease, you should ask your landlord if they would be offering a discounted rent program. If your landlord has not heard of a discounted rent program, you can offer to educate them. It can be a win-win situation for both you and the landlord.

If the rent asked for is $450 a month and is due on the 1st and late on the 5th or 10th, ask for a discount if you pay the rent a little early or exactly on time. Most landlords spend the first 10-20 days of the month trying to collect all of the rent. They worry about it a lot.

You can offer to pay your rent by the 1st of the month or by the 31st of the previous month—not on the 5th or 10th like many tenants do. In exchange for paying the landlord early and assuring them that they do not have to worry about when your rent is coming, you ask for, and should get a discount of anywhere from $20-$100/month.

> **Example:** Your rent is $450 a month and is due on the 1st and late on the 6th. Negotiate with your landlord to pay the rent a little early and get a discount. You can agree to pay or mail the rent on the 30th of the previous month and get a $25 discount or pay $425. Your landlord has bills to pay and should appreciate the opportunity to receive the rent a little early and in a more predictable manner. If your rent is $850/month, you should be able to negotiate a larger discount, i.e., pay $790 by the 1st of the month. That is a $60 discount, which in a year adds up to $720 in savings!

When Negotiating Discounted Rent

1. Only negotiate for discounted rent after you have politely tried to ask for the lowest rent possible. Ask for free months of rent first. Next, ask for the lowest rent possible. Then inquire about any discounts on rent for cleaning, painting and repairs. Finally, after you have arrived at the best rent possible, start talking about discounted rent. You would not want to get a discount on a higher rent, because that discount is not really a true savings for you!

2. Do not ask for a discounted rate savings if you are not comfortable that you will be able to pay your rent early. Perhaps you receive your paycheck on the 3rd or 5th of the month, and are unable to make an early rent payment. Be sure that you really can pay the rent a little early.

3. Always get all agreements in writing. If you do successfully negotiate a discounted rent program that will save you money, get it in writing. Make sure that you and your landlord sign it, date it, and that all of the terms are absolutely clear. Please keep copies of all agreements you sign, including leases, discounted rent forms, and anything else that you and your landlord agree to.

Some people take the discounted rent approach to the next level. If you have extra cash or are receiving a lump sum of money, you may want to consider pre-paying a few months, six months or maybe even a year's worth of rent up front. However, make sure you can afford to do it. Also make sure that your discount or savings is worth it. If you earn 8% on your money in an investment such as a mutual fund or money market fund, then you would want at least an 8% savings on your rent.

> **Example:** Your rent is $600/month. You offer to pre-pay 6 months' rent. You should get a nice discount for doing this. You pay 6 x $540 or $3,240 instead of the $3,600 you would have paid. This is about a 10% discount. Your landlord may really like this as they could probably use the money now. But remember:

- Do not do it if you have a better use for the cash, e.g., it earns 12% in a mutual fund.
- Get a written receipt for the rent you paid.
- Be sure that you trust the landlord you are handing over so much money to.
- This can be a great way to get ahead on your bills.
- Be doubly sure that you can afford to part with this much cash.

Clean or Paint for Discounted Rent and/or Deposit

How often have you gone to rent a place and have found it has not been painted, needs cleaning, or has some repairs that need to be done? Often, landlords do not have the repair people to get all of the work done, or at least might appreciate it if they did not have to worry about getting the work done. If you are able and willing to do a bit of cleaning and/or painting, you could negotiate some big discounts on your rent and deposit. If you are looking for a discount, but are shown an already clean unit, ask if they have one that needs some work.

3

Putting in a Better Application

Finally, you have found the right place, but you are still a little stressed. You know that you will most likely have to put in an application, but you are worried that your application may not be good enough. Perhaps you found the place you want, but so have three other people who also want to rent it. By following the advice given in this section, you will be able to improve your application and better your chances of getting the place you want.

What is the Landlord really looking for?

Put yourself for just a moment in the landlord's place. What they really want is very simple!

- To have someone move into their place who can and will pay the rent.
- To have a tenant who will not cause any problems for

21

the landlord or the neighbors.
- To have a tenant who will take good care of the house or apartment.
- To find a tenant stable enough to stay for at least one year, but even better, to stay for many years. Every time a tenant moves, it is very expensive for the landlord because of lost rent while the apartment is vacant and repair costs to get the place ready for someone else.

Remember to give the landlord what they are looking for when you apply for your new home. Do everything that you can to convince the landlord that you can and will pay the rent on time, not bother anyone, take care of the property, and stay for a long time. Of course, you must do all this sincerely and honestly.

First Impressions Count

Just as when you meet anyone, first impressions with a potential landlord are very important. When you speak on the phone with them or see them in person, try to abide by the following checklist.

1. Be friendly, polite, and speak clearly.

2. Maintain eye contact.

3. Dress as professionally and neatly as possible. Dress as if you are going to one of the most important business meetings of your life. After all, you may be living in this place for the next few years of your life.

4. Do not have a lot of background noise on the phone when you are speaking. Children, T.V., stereo, etc., should all be quiet or in another room if possible.

5. Do not take friends or relatives with you into an interview, unless it is for your security (you are viewing an empty unit or stand alone house).

6. If you are with friends or relatives, make sure they are dressed neatly and conduct themselves politely. People often judge us by the company we keep.

7. Try not to chew gum or eat while speaking.

8. If you arrive in a car, make sure it is clean and tidy. Some landlords take note of your car. They may think that how you keep your car shows them how you keep your house.

9. If children are with you, make sure that they remain well-behaved and are also dressed neatly. Many a good tenant has been turned down for a rental property because one of their children began destroying the apartment during the application process.

10. Be prepared. Anticipate what the landlord will ask for and have it ready. In the next section you will learn how to do this and with a little bit of effort on your part, you will be better prepared than all of the others there. Unless, of course, they've read the *Renter's Handbook* too!

> **Example:** say you are applying for a new apartment. There is a lot of demand in your area for apartments, so you know that you are not the only one applying. If you make a good first impression, don't you think that your chances of getting the place you want will be greatly increased? Some people might think that the above checklist is too simple. As a landlord, I can tell you that many people have shown up to rent one of my places drunk, pants unzipped, with food hanging out of their mouths; have let their children draw on the walls while they put in an application, and drove cars full of beer cans which fell out when they opened

the door! Don't underestimate the importance of the first impression.

Prepare Yourself to be the Best Applicant

With just a little effort, you can prepare yourself to put in a good application. The first step is to gather all the information that you are going to need to answer the landlord's questions.

1. Your current address
2. Previous addresses for the last 7 years or so, and the length of time you lived at each one
3. Your previous landlord's name, address, and phone number
4. Your current employer

Impress Any Landlord

If you really want to impress a landlord, fill out and create an application folder or booklet. Go to your local office supply store and get a folder or binder with a clear cover. Put a cover sheet on it with your name typewritten and include:

1. Your resume
2. A sample application already filled out
3. A letter from your employer verifying employment
4. A copy of your W-2 or something showing your job and income
5. Letters of reference (if they are good) from previous landlords
6. Letters of reference from employers, teachers, religious leaders, etc.
7. A copy of your credit report

Most landlords will ask for some, if not all, of these

things. Why not anticipate what they want and have it all ready. Think how organized and efficient you'd look! You still may have to fill out their application, but at the very least you will have all of your information ready and you will impress the landlord. If three or four or more people are applying for the same place, you may be setting yourself apart from them by your dress and manner and by presenting a neat and well-organized folder filled with the information your landlord is looking for. Try it! You will impress the landlord and greatly improve your chances of getting the place you really want.

Fair Housing: It's The Law

When you apply for a new house or apartment, your application should be reviewed based upon criteria that the landlord has. The first person who applies and meets those criteria should have their application approved.

According to the Federal Fair Housing Amendments Act of 1988, no one may discriminate in the sale or rental of housing because of:
• race
• color
• national origin
• religion
• sex
• familial status (including children under the age of 18 living with parents or legal custodians; pregnant women and people securing custody of children under the age of 18).
• handicap (someone with a physical or mental disability including hearing, mobility and visual impairments, chronic alcoholism, chronic mental illness, AIDS, AIDS related complex, and mental retardation).

If you do have a handicap, a landlord cannot refuse to let you make reasonable modifications to a place or the common use area at your expense. A landlord may require

25

that you put the place back in its original condition if you modified the unit due to your handicap.

You should report any hint of discrimination to your local fair housing office, which may be housed in the HUD (U.S. Department of Housing and Urban Development— see appendix for addresses and telephone numbers).

You must be treated equally and fairly and cannot be discriminated against. This includes seeing a place, applying for a place, negotiating for a place, being screened for a place, and setting terms and conditions of your renting a place. If you feel that you are being treated differently by a landlord or potential landlord because of your race, color, origin, religion, sex, familial status or handicap, contact your nearest fair housing office at once.

Your Credit Report

So many people are worried about their credit, especially if they are looking for a new place to live. Many people will not even look for place, perhaps even choosing to remain in an unacceptable situation (a bad neighborhood, a place with a lot of maintenance problems, etc.,) because they know that they will have to endure "the dreaded credit check." You may be worried because, like many renters, your credit is not perfect and you do not want it checked. Well, worry no more! Read on and learn some of the truth about your credit, how it really affects your chances of being accepted into a place, and how you can take action to help your credit, help yourself, and increase your chances of getting the place you really want.

Get a copy of your credit report today. A large percentage of credit reports contain errors. Even if you think that you have perfect credit, get a copy of your credit report so that you can be sure.

If you are worried about your credit and you think it is not perfect or it is bad, please get a copy of your report to see how it really looks. You should do this once a year to make sure there are no errors.

How to Get a Copy of your Credit Report

Call one of the three major credit reporting bureaus. If you have been denied credit recently, you may be able to get a free copy of your credit report. If you have not been denied credit, you may have to send the agency $8-10 for a copy of your report. The major reporting agencies are:

TRW 1-800-392-1122
TransUnion 1-316-636-6100
Equifax 1-800-685-1111

Not only should they send you a copy of your credit report, they should also send you a guide to help you understand your report. Generally, you will see your name, address, employer, and then a list of any accounts or creditors you have. If you pay that bill on time, you will get a "1". If you pay the bill within 30-59 days, you will get a "2". If you pay the bill 60-89 days after it is due, you will get a "3". If a bill goes to a collection agency, you will get a "9". Check everything on your credit report: there could be mistakes.

If you have a mistake on your credit report and a mistake can be anything from an exact amount, a wrong date, to a wrong account number you can challenge it.

Know Your Rights

The Fair Credit Reporting Act of 1970 gives you some basic rights. Many people are not aware of these rights and pay hundreds of dollars to "credit repair" companies. You can know your rights and take action on your own and possibly save hundreds of dollars and improve your credit. You have the right to:

1. See your credit report for free. If you have been

denied credit in the last 30 days, you are entitled to a free copy of your credit report. You can and should get a copy of your credit report. If you have not been denied credit, you will be charged $8-10. Request your copy today!

2. Dispute any errors. If you dispute any errors, the credit bureaus must under Federal Law research any items on your credit report that you believe to be incorrect.

3. File a written statement giving your account of what happened. If you have a good reason as to why you got behind on a bill, you can put it in writing and it will be attached to your credit report.

You can dispute any errors on your credit report and the credit bureau has a "reasonable time" to investigate and confirm what is on your report. This "reasonable time" is about 30 days. If the credit bureau deems your claim to be "frivolous or irrelevant," it does not have to investigate the matter. However, the bureaus very rarely deem matters to be frivolous as they have been to court many times on these matters. If the bureau finds an error, or cannot confirm something positively that you have challenged, they will most likely remove it from your credit report.

Most Common Errors on a Credit Report

- Other people's accounts on your report.
- Accounts that are seven years and older that should have been removed. Note: a Chapter 7 bankruptcy which completely discharges all of your unsecured debts remains on your credit report for 10 years. A Chapter 13 filing, which takes your debt and restructures it into a debt repayment plan, should be erased from your record after 7 years. If you find these types of judgement, they should be removed.

The Renter's Credit Repair Plan
1. Obtain a Copy of Your Credit Report. Study it for any errors. *Any* errors. If you owed $829 and the report says $842, that is an error. Check dates, amounts, numbers, names, etc.

2. If you find an error, immediately write a letter stating what is in error. Send the letter to the credit bureau certified, return receipt requested. The letter should look something like this:

To: Credit Bureau
From: Your Name
Re: My Credit Report
Date:

Your Name, Address, Social Security Number, and Telephone Number

My credit report contains what I believe to be the following errors.

— I have never had an account with _____ company.

— The amount on the account listed as _____ is not correct.

— This _____ company, account number was not mine. The account number is wrong.

Please remove these items from my credit reports. I look forward to hearing from you soon.

Thank you.

Your Name

Remember

- **Write as you would speak.** If your have trouble writing it, just say it as you would to a friend, and then write down what you said.
- **Keep a copy of the mailing receipt and the letter.** If you do not hear from the credit bureau within about 30 days, send another letter stating that "this is your second letter. The first one was sent on _____ (date)." The credit bureau should respond within about 30 days. If they do not, you could possibly have a case against them.
- **Be honest.**

Many "credit repair" companies that charge hundreds of dollars claim that the credit bureaus do not have the ability to verify all of the "disputed items" so that some items that you dispute will perhaps be removed. This may or may not be true, but if there is an error it should be taken off your report and sometimes, especially if an account is older, the bureau may have trouble verifying the information and may remove it. If your claims are legitimate and you do it in writing, you have nothing to lose.

3. Verify with the creditor. Contact the original creditor in writing. If the credit bureau reports that you have a late bill or unpaid debt with XYZ Co., contact XYZ Co. Try to verify the information with them. If there is a mistake, go back to the credit bureau. Try also to work out a payment plan with the original creditor, and have them notify the credit bureau and remove the item.

4. If the bureau for some reason will not remove an "incorrect item" from your report, contact in writing the Better Business Bureau for your state, your State Attorney General's Office and the Federal Trade Commission (see appendix).

If an incorrect item is not removed in a "reasonable

time" you could also have a very good lawsuit. Consult an attorney if the above measures have not brought you satisfaction.

5. Get your account of what happened on the record. If the information is on your credit report, you can file up to a 100-word explanation of what has happened. File the explanation with the credit bureau and they should include it when people look at your credit report. You should do this if you have a legitimate reason or excuse as to why you have an unpaid or late bill that is on your credit report. Instead of explaining to every landlord and all of your other potential creditors why there is a mark on your credit, you should put it in writing and have the explanation become a part of your credit report.

Many landlords might dismiss or deny you a place because you have some bad credit. If you have a legitimate excuse and it is part of your credit report, many landlords and creditors may understand and give your application a good, hard second look if they know why you had some problems.

Example A: Your credit report shows that you were 60 days late on some bills. Your credit is not great, so your application for a new place is denied.

Example B: Your credit report shows that you were 60 days late on some bills. Your report also has a 100 word explanation telling how you were very sick for a few months, got behind, but have now been feeling well and are caught up on your bills. Or: that at some period you were laid off from work through no fault of your own and that you have now found employment and are caught up.

Most people, landlords included, have had themselves or know someone who has had hard times before. With a good, honest, legitimate explanation of why your credit is not great, many landlords may give you a break . Include these explanations in any application folder you prepare.

If you do not have bad credit, emphasize your positive credit to the landlord. What are landlords really interested in? Whether or not you are going to pay the rent on time. Many people do not pay all of their bills on time and as a result have bad credit. However, those very people may always pay their rent on time. If you are such a person, point it out in writing to your landlord that you pay your rent on time. Written evidence or copies of cancelled checks for the last six months or year will really help. Try to include all of this in your application folder.

Bankruptcy

Unfortunately, many people who have had serious credit problems have declared bankruptcy. Many of these people are afraid to move or worried that they will never have their application approved. True, many landlords will not permit someone who has a recent bankruptcy on their credit report to rent one of their properties. However, you can help educate landlords as to the facts and help yourself to have your application possibly approved regardless of the fact that you have a bankruptcy on your record.

Myth: *People who just went bankrupt always make bad tenants.*

Fact: Some people who have declared bankruptcy make great tenants and they may be able to pay the rent very well. In a Chapter 7 bankruptcy, all unsecured debts are probably discharged. This enables the person declaring bankruptcy to have a fresh start. You may want to inform your potential landlord that you now have very little, if any, debt to pay. Of course, ethically and morally, all debts should be repaid and this is in no way a recommendation that anyone should declare bankruptcy. The reality is that many people have and will declare bankruptcy, so landlords should be informed that they may not make bad tenants.

Myth: People who declared bankruptcy will not pay their bills and will declare bankruptcy again.
Fact: People who have declared bankruptcy cannot declare bankruptcy again more than once every six years. You should inform your potential landlord that not only do you have a fresh start, but that you will have to be responsible for your rent and debts as you cannot declare bankruptcy again for six years after your last bankruptcy. Other renters can declare bankruptcy and delay or avoid their rent and debts for a long time and possibly even wipe out a landlord's claims through a bankruptcy.

Myth: Once a person has declared bankruptcy, they are labeled for life and they will never be given credit again, let alone be allowed to rent a new place.
Fact: Some creditors and many landlords will work with people who have declared bankruptcy for the above mentioned reasons: you have a fresh start, and you cannot declare bankruptcy again for six years. If you have declared bankruptcy, you are not alone. The American Bankruptcy Institute estimates that between 1990 and 1995 there were 32.3 bankruptcy filings per 1,000 people in the United States. There are many people who have declared bankruptcy who soon afterwards rent new places, buy homes, and get credit again. Some lenders look for and advertise for people who have declared bankruptcy as they understand that many people who have declared bankruptcy make great new borrowers.

Myth: A potential landlord will never understand how you could go bankrupt.
Fact: Many people have declared bankruptcy for some fairly legitimate reasons and you may be one of them. If your bankruptcy has an understandable explanation, like a layoff from work, illness, death in the family, divorce, or

some other "good reason," let the landlord know. Attach the reason in writing to your credit report if you can, or put an explanation in your Application Folder.

Landlords are people too, and many of them may understand your situation if you give them the opportunity. Without providing them and your other potential creditors or lenders the information, you will never know if they will understand. Give them the chance. Give yourself the chance. You have nothing to lose.

Establishing Your Credit

It is hard to get credit if you have no credit. If you have no credit and want to establish credit, or re-establish credit, you could consider the following:

1. If offered a credit card, accept it. Charge on it only what you can afford, and pay it off before the due date. This will establish your credit. Please make sure you understand all of the responsibilities and risks of getting a credit card.

2. Apply for a secured credit card. This is a credit card that is secured by money that you have on deposit with the credit card company.

> **Example:** You deposit $500 in a bank and that bank gives you a credit card with a limit of $500 or the amount secured by the bank account.

3. Department Store Cards. These are generally easier to get than a regular credit card. Apply for one.

4. Gas Company Cards. Again, this may be a good starting place.

5. Secured Bank or Finance Company Loans. Many

people have established credit by depositing $100 in a bank, borrowing $50, paying it back, and then increasing the amount.

6. Buying Items on Time. Many stores and mail order catalogs allow you to get on a payment plan. Check with them to see if they report to the credit bureaus. If they do, this may help you to establish your credit.

Warnings!!
1. Never charge anything that you cannot afford. It is always preferable to pay all credit cards and loans off in full without incurring the usually high finance charges. As my grandfather taught me, if you cannot pay for it now, you do not need it now.

2. The number of times that your credit is checked, or the number of applications you make for credit will most likely show up on your credit report. If many applications are made, your credit may be negatively affected. Companies do not generally like to see numerous applications for credit in a short period of time. Do your homework and try to determine if you will be accepted before you apply. This is also true for landlords. Remember, in your application package you have a copy of your credit report, and all of your background and references. Let the landlord look at this and then politely ask what your chances are of being accepted before they run a new credit check.

Application and Credit Enhancers
If, after attempting all of the methods in this chapter, you still do not feel that your application is good enough, there is more you can do. Perhaps your credit is really bad, you have no credit at all or you have had trouble paying your rent in the past. You can attempt to make many of these problems unimportant if you can get **a co-signer** who

does have great credit.

Most people know someone who has a good income, good savings and good credit. It may be a family member, a close friend, employer, religious leader, counselor, business or agency they are affiliated with, or a rich uncle! Many a landlord can be convinced to let you move in if they are assured that one way or another they will get their rent, either from you or from your well-off co-signer.

A co-signer is someone who also signs the lease and is responsible for paying the rent and any other conditions of the lease that they co-sign. Please make sure that your potential co-signer is aware of the responsibilities and risks of co-signing. If you cannot pay the rent, then they must pay it. They may also, depending on what the lease says, have to pay for any damage that you cause to the rental apartment or house.

If your credit is not great or the landlord does not seem to be enthused about renting to you because of something on your application, but you really want the place, you can offer to:

1. Put down a much larger security deposit than required. If the landlord is hesitant about renting to you, offer a larger security deposit.

Example: You want to rent a new place. The advertisement said $545/month with a $350 deposit. After you negotiate for the best deal possible and present your application presentation folder, the landlord says that your credit is not good enough to be accepted. If you can afford it and really want the place, offer to put a deposit of $450 or a full month's rent, $545, as a deposit. You should emphasize that this should make the landlord feel more comfortable and increase your chances of getting the place.

2. Offer to pay more rent than is being asked. This is risky, as you are effectively wasting the extra money every month. Also, be sure you can afford to pay the extra amount. Any good landlord would probably at least listen to your offer and might reconsider your application.

3. Have the full amount, rent and deposit, available when you apply. Landlords like the fact that they could get their money today and not in two or three weeks.

4. Offer to pre-pay a few months of rent in advance. A not-so-great application may look a lot better if you pre-pay some of the rent. The reason the landlord is worried about your application is your ability to pay the rent. If you pre-pay some of it, then the landlord's worries will be greatly reduced and your chances of getting the place you want will be increased. Again, be sure that you can afford to pre-pay the rent and get all agreements in writing with receipts showing that you have pre-paid the rent.

> **Example:** You want a place, but the landlord does not want to approve your application or has already denied it. The landlord wants $595/month rent. You offer to pre-pay three month's rent in advance to make the landlord feel more comfortable renting to you. Be sure your offer is in dollars. Offer to pre-pay or to pay the landlord 3 x $595 = $1,785 now. This offer should get the landlord's attention.

5. Offer to fix up, or help paint and clean a place that is not ready. This will save the landlord a lot of money and show them that you care about the place.

Make the landlord feel comfortable with you, your ability to pay, and your ability to take care of the place. Everything you say, do, and present to the landlord should be geared towards positively proving these things to the landlord. Try the above mentioned techniques. Anticipate and answer all of the landlord's concerns before they are raised. Set yourself apart from the other applicants with your application presentation folder. The best of luck to you in getting the place you want!

Application Checklist

❑ Filled out a sample application so you will have most if not all of the information you need ready (typewritten if possible).

❑ Obtained and reviewed a copy of your credit report.

❑ Have references in writing from previous landlords.

❑ Have personal references in writing from employers, religious leaders, and other people who can vouch for your good character.

❑ Verification of employment

❑ Verification of income. Copies of W-2s, pay stubs, etc.

❑ Verification of bank accounts, savings plans, investments, etc., showing you have money.

❑ All of the above presented attractively in an application folder.

❑ Check your appearance before meeting a potential landlord.

4

Screening Your Landlord

Before you decide to move into a place, you should remember that not only are you renting an apartment or house that you must check out and screen carefully, but you are also about to begin a long term relationship with a new landlord. You should make sure that landlord is someone you really want to have a relationship with. We all know that landlords screen tenants. Don't you think tenants should screen landlords? Besides thoroughly inspecting the unit before you move in, you should:

1. Talk to at Least Two Neighbors. Ask them how they like living there and how they are being treated by the landlord. Remember, though, that everyone has different opinions. For instance, you may like a movie and your best friend may think it is awful. In the same way, you may love your landlord and your neighbors may hate him! However, it is good to ask, and if you never ask you will

never know. Some questions to ask the neighbors are:
- **How do they like living there?**
- **What do they like best about the place?**
- **What do they like least about the place?**
- **Is the area safe and quiet?**
- **What kind of people live here?**
- **How long does it take to get something fixed?**
- **Is the landlord a good landlord, and why?**

2. Interview Your Landlord. Do it in a pleasant and businesslike way. If they are professional and care about what they do, they should not mind answering your questions. Be sure first that they have time to talk. If they are busy, schedule a later time that is good for both of you.

- **Ask the landlord how long they have managed the property.** If they are new, ask why.
- **Ask them who is responsible for collecting the rent.**
- **Ask them who is responsible for doing the repairs.** Since getting things repaired in a timely manner seems to be one of the major complaints that tenants have about their landlords, you should ask about your prospective landlord's repair policies and procedures:
  a) Who do you call for repairs?
  b) Who will then be in charge and responsible for the repairs?
  c) How long does it usually take once you call for them to fix a leaking faucet?
- **Ask them how many apartments and/or houses they manage.** If it is a lot, more than 50, ask them how many people work for them. Who is available in the case of an emergency? And on the weekend?
- **Ask them what they like and do not like about managing properties.**

All of these questions will help you determine the experience, professionalism and attitude of your potential landlord. If they have a lot of experience and seem to be positive about their job, then it is more likely that they will be a good landlord.

Please remember that you should only ask these questions *after* you have been approved, or after you have made a favorable impression on your potential landlord. If you start asking these questions the first second you meet the landlord, they may misinterpret your interest and think that you break a lot of things!

3. Be aware of how your landlord and their office responds to your phone calls.
- **Did they return your calls quickly?** (If they do not return your calls now they may not return them if you move in).
- **Were they pleasant on the phone?**
- **Did they answer all of your questions?**
  And most importantly:
- **Do they seem to care?**

If the rental office does not return your calls, treat you politely or seem to care now when they are supposed to be "selling" you on a new place to live, they probably will not make any effort to be nice to you later when you have moved in and have a real problem.

If you are looking for a new place to live, you are probably more than a little stressed out. You may need to find a place to live right away! Please don't rush into renting a place only to regret it later. Take a few extra minutes and interview your landlord. Remember, most leases are for a year. Spare yourself twelve months of potential misery by finding out now, before you sign, what the people running the place are like. You will be dealing with them for the next year.

Screen Your Landlord Test

The following is a guide for interviewing your landlord. It tells you some of the actions you can take to screen your landlord effectively. It can help you determine whether the landlord is, or will be, great, good, or horrible!

Keep in mind that one of the most important attributes of a good landlord is that they care about you and their property. If your potential landlord seems to care, then you will probably have fewer problems with them. No one is perfect, but with a little planning and preparation, you *can* avoid renting from "the landlord from Hell".

1. The potential landlord returned your phone call:

a) within 12 hours	_____	(5)
b) within 24 hours	_____	(4)
c) within 2 days	_____	(3)
d) after 3 days or more	_____	(2)
e) did not return your phone call	_____	(0)

2. When you first spoke to them, they were:

a) polite and friendly	_____	(5)
b) just businesslike	_____	(4)
c) short and impatient	_____	(3)
d) not interested in talking to you	_____	(2)
e) rude and impolite	_____	(0)

3. Their office and/or the place where you met them was:

a) very neat, orderly and clean	_____	(5)
b) nice, but cluttered	_____	(4)
c) adequate	_____	(3)
d) not very nice	_____	(2)
e) dirty and dingy	_____	(0)

4. You spoke to two neighbors who currently rent from
  the landlord and they told you:
   a) the landlord was great and
    they love living there   ____ (5)
   b) one said the landlord was
    great and the other said the
    landlord was just ok   ____ (4)
   c) both neighbors said the landlord
    was pretty good, but they mentioned
    some minor problems   ____ (3)
   d) both neighbors said the landlord was
    pretty bad, but did take care of most
    things   ____ (2)
   e) both neighbors said the landlord was
    bad and/or they are moving   ____ (0)

5. The property you are looking at is:
   a) really nice, neat, clean and looks
    great   ____ (5)
   b) pretty clean and seems well kept   ____ (4)
   c) ok, but has some minor defects   ____ (3)
   d) a little trashy and seems to need
    some work   ____ (2)
   e) is dirty, not repaired, and trashy   ____ (0)

Now add up your prospective landlord's scores.

Between 23 and 25. Excellent. A great potential landlord.
Between 19 and 22. Good. Could be a nice landlord.
Between 13 and 18. Average. You may want to check them out a little more.
Between 9 and 12. Be careful. You may have a below average landlord.
8 and under. Danger! You may be talking to the landlord from hell!

5

Understanding Your Lease

Warning: Read This Before You Sign

In this chapter, you will find out what is in the lease and what to watch out for. You will also learn what a lease really is and why you should have one.

A lease is a contract between you, the renter, and the landlord. Just like any contract, you need to read it and understand what the contract says before you sign it. It is estimated that over 85% of renters never read their lease. You need to be in the percentile that not only read their lease, but understand it!

A lease, like any other contract, sets out the duties and responsibilities of each party to the contract. The landlord lets you occupy and use the "leased property" in exchange for rent. Usually, the lease has a lot of other duties/responsibilities and things that you need to be aware of and watch out for.

Most basic leases will contain the following:

44

- Names of the landlord and renter.
- The address of the rental property.
- The amount of rent.
- When the rent is due and the late charges.
- How to get out of the lease. That is, the length of time of the lease.
- The security deposit.
- What the landlord will provide in the way of utilities, services, and other amenities like a pool or laundry.
- The responsibilities of the tenant.
- Regulations and rules that constitute grounds for eviction.
- What the landlord is supposed to do.

Many renters never sign a lease, have no written lease, or have a lease that has expired, e.g., they signed a one-year lease three years ago and have never renewed it. If you are one of these people, guess what? You probably still have a lease even if it is not in writing. Most states recognize what is called a tenant at will. In many states, even if you have no written agreement but are renting with the landlord's permission, you may still be protected by your state landlord/tenant laws. In other words, if you do not have a written lease, the state may imply one for you.

Many problems occur when there is no written lease as the landlord and/or the tenant are not certain of their duties and responsibilities. You should find comfort in the fact that in many areas the state or city landlord/tenant laws give you some protection. Generally, a landlord and tenant can agree in a written lease to terminate or end the lease at any time. In many states, if you do not have a written lease and are a "tenant at will," you will probably have some protection such as a reasonable amount of notice to leave or vacate the property. Usually, you should receive at least a 30 day written notice. Similarly, if you want to end or terminate a "tenancy at will," you will be required to give the landlord reasonable notice. In many areas of the country, if you do not have a written lease and pay by the month, you are deemed to have a "month to month" lease and must be given a month's notice to move. If you pay weekly, you may have a "week to week" lease and only have a seven day notice period to have your lease terminated. All notices should be given in writing. If your landlord tells you to move in three days, you legally may have a right to a 30 day written notice even if you do not have a written lease. (See the appendix for the state rulings on the amount of notice required to terminate a month-to-month tenancy.)

Remember, every city and state is different. Consult the appendix to find out more about your area's laws.

Now, since you may have some rights even without a written lease, you may be wondering why have a written lease at all? There are some definite advantages to having a written lease. The advantages are that the landlord's and tenant's duties are spelled out clearly and are more verifiable if they are in writing. If there is a problem or dispute concerning your agreement to rent, how long it was for, how much, who was to provide what, etc., it is certainly better to have a written lease or agreement. So many landlord/tenant problems are caused because "the landlord said I could..." Get it in writing. A lease is the way to do it.

Another important advantage of getting a written lease is that your rent payment will be fixed for a definite time. If you have a 12 month lease for a monthly rent payment of $595, then your rent is fixed for one year. If you do not have a written lease, and you have a month to month lease, your rent can probably be raised with a 30 day notice. If you wanted to, you could negotiate for a 6 month, one-year, two-year, or even a five-year lease with a fixed rental payment ensuring that your rent will not go up for the agreed length of time. Be sure that you really want to stay in your place for the length of time that you specify!

Of course, if you only want to rent for a short time and/or do not want to be bound by a lot of agreements, you may not want a written lease. However, as you will discover as you read on, it is possible to put into a lease what you want and need.

Most renters will sign a lease thinking that all leases are the same. They are not. Most people will sign any agreement thinking that it is a "standard agreement" and it must be O.K. Rest assured, it is not O.K.

Many landlords spend a lot of time and money on attorney's fees, drafting leases and agreements that, believe it or not, are not in favor of you, the renter. You need to understand exactly what you are signing and agreeing to. If you do not understand and agree with it, do not sign it.

What To Do If You Want to Change Something In A Lease

You may be saying to yourself that there is no choice. You must sign the lease as it is or you will not be able to rent the new place you have found. This is not the case. All agreements, including all leases, can be modified. You do not agree with everything you are told. Sometimes, you may disagree with someone or something and arrive at a compromise. The same can be true of your lease. You can have the landlord explain a clause you do not understand or agree with. Then, you can politely discuss your concerns about the part of the lease that you are not comfortable with and modify it. A modification is a change to a lease. Any and all changes must be

• in writing
• attached to the lease
• initialed and signed by both you and the landlord

You can actually change some words or a phrase or two on the lease, by marking out the words you do not agree with and putting your own words in.

Example:

In your lease, it says that "the tenant must give a 60 day notice to terminate the lease." You scratch out the 60 and put 30 or 20 or 45, whatever you feel comfortable with, then you and the landlord both initial the change and make sure the lease is signed.

Remember: speak with and negotiate with your landlord before changing or modifying your lease or rental agreement.

Your landlord should explain and help you understand your lease before you sign it. If they cannot, will not, or do not explain it to you and you do not understand parts of your lease, please get help in understanding your lease before you sign it. Ask a friend, family member, speak with an attorney or contact the National Association for Renter's Rights so that you understand what you are signing.

Watch Out for The Landlord's Illegal Trick

Generally, you cannot agree to something in a lease that is not legal. For instance, some landlords, because of lack of knowledge, mistakenly using old form leases, or because they want to play an illegal trick, may have clauses in their leases that violate your area's landlord/tenant laws. For instance, in almost all states, you can only be evicted or removed from your home or apartment by a court action. Some landlords have clauses in their leases requiring that you must leave if you are five days late on the rent or the landlord tells you to. This clause or agreement in your lease probably has no real meaning as it most likely violates a statutory law.

Besides, you should be reviewing and understanding your lease so that you would not agree to or sign such a lease anyway. You would mark it out or modify it, have the landlord and yourself initial the change(s), and sign and date the lease. You can also add an amendment signed by you and and the landlord (see next page for example).

The Landlord Will Not Rent To You If You Complain About The Lease

Perhaps you are worried that your landlord or potential landlord will be upset if you question their lease. First of all, signing a lease or any agreement is a big deal. Most leases are for a year, so you will probably have to live with this lease for a year or so of your life. It is important to take the time to completely understand, discuss, and agree to your lease. If your landlord will not take the time now to help you understand your lease before you sign it, then you may want to reconsider renting from them. They probably will not be responsive at all six months from now when you need help with a repair or some other problem. If you are reasonable in your questions and requests about the lease, so should the landlord be in responding to them.

Sample Amendment to Lease or Rental Agreement

This is an Amendment to the lease or rental agreement dated

_____ 199___ (the Agreement between)

<u>Larry Landlord</u> ("Landlord") and

<u>Rob Renter</u> ("Tenant") regarding property located at

<u>588 Rentright St, Anytown</u> ("the premises")

49

Landlord and Tenant agree to the following changes and/or additions to the Agreement:

1. Beginning June 1 1997, Tenant shall rent a one-car garage, adjacent to the main premises from landlord for the sum of $75 per month.

2. Tenant may keep one German Shepherd Dog on the premises . The dog shall be kept on a leash in the yard unless tenant is present. Tenant shall clean up all animal waste from the yard on a daily basis. Tenant agrees to repair any damages to the yard or premises caused by his dog, at tenant's expense.

Signed: <u>Larry Landlord</u>   Date: May 20 1997
        Landlord

Signed: <u>Rob Renter</u>   Date: May 20 1997
        Tenant

50

6

Move In / Move Out Checklist

Why You Need To Complete This Checklist

Completing a checklist when you move in and out of a rental property is crucial for the following reasons:

1. It can help you to get your security deposit back. In order to get your security deposit back, you should be able to show that you are leaving the rental unit as you found it. Tenants are generally only responsible for damage beyond fair wear and tear. With a move-in inspection sheet, you can help protect your rights when the time comes for you to try to get your security deposit back.

2. It can help you avoid problems when you move. So many problems, headaches and ill-will arise because a unit was not inspected thoroughly before someone move in. So often, renters will rent a place without seeing it or inspecting it. Then, when they do move in, they become frustrated because something does not work, does not look like it should, the carpet is dirty or old, the shower does not work, or it is simply not what they expected. Inspect the unit and do not move into it until it is really ready. Save yourself a lot of hassles and perhaps a lot of money, too. If you move in without inspecting the property, you might have to move again and that could cost you big money. Inspect, be happy!

	Move In	**Move Out**
Living Room		
Door (incl. locks)	_____	_____
Windows	_____	_____
Carpet or Floor	_____	_____
Walls	_____	_____
Ceiling	_____	_____
Lights & Switches	_____	_____
Other	_____	_____
Dining Room		
Windows	_____	_____
Carpet or Floor	_____	_____
Walls	_____	_____
Ceiling	_____	_____
Lights & Switches	_____	_____
Other	_____	_____
Hallway		
Floor	_____	_____
Walls	_____	_____
Ceiling	_____	_____
Other	_____	_____

Kitchen

Windows _____ _____
Floor _____ _____
Walls _____ _____
Ceiling _____ _____
Lights & Switches _____ _____
Stove _____ _____
Refrigerator _____ _____
Sink _____ _____
Cabinets & Counters _____ _____
Other _____ _____

Bedroom

Door _____ _____
Windows _____ _____
Carpet or Floor _____ _____
Walls _____ _____
Ceiling _____ _____
Lights & Switches _____ _____
Closet _____ _____
Other _____ _____

Bathroom

Door _____ _____
Windows _____ _____
Carpet or Floor _____ _____
Walls _____ _____
Ceiling _____ _____
Lights & Switches _____ _____
Sink _____ _____
Tub/Shower _____ _____
Toilet _____ _____
Cabinet, Shelves _____ _____
Closet _____ _____
Towel Bars _____ _____
Other _____ _____

Furniture Inventory (Use this if rental unit is furnished. Check condition of items and number present)

	Move In	Move Out
Kitchen chairs	_____	_____
Tables	_____	_____
End Tables	_____	_____
Lounge chairs	_____	_____
Sofas	_____	_____
Lamps	_____	_____
Desks	_____	_____
Desk Chairs	_____	_____
Bookcases	_____	_____
Mattresses	_____	_____
Dressers	_____	_____

Signature of Tenants	_____
Address of Property	_____
Signature of Landlord	_____
Landlord's Address	_____
Phone Number	_____
Date	_____

7

Protecting Yourself

Security and safety are issues for everyone in every town now. These recommendations may help you be a little safer both when you are looking for a new place to live and after you have moved in. Much of this may sound obvious, but so few of us do it. Here are some things you can do to protect yourself when looking for a place to live and once you have moved in.

Safety Tips When Looking for a New Apartment or House

Looking for a new apartment or house can sometimes be a risky business. If you are new to town, or are unfamiliar with a certain area, you may be concerned about straying into problem neighborhoods where you may not be as safe as you would like to be. Even if you know your way around a city or neighborhood, you may still be putting yourself at risk by arranging to meet with total strangers in order to look at vacant properties. Be careful and always trust your instincts. If a particular situation or individual makes you feel uncomfortable, leave. Keep the following suggestions in mind when looking for a new apartment or house.

1. Never meet anyone in a vacant apartment or house alone. Take a friend or relative with you. If the landlord does not have a rental office that you can go to, be sure that the person you are meeting is reputable. Get a description of who you are meeting. Do not get out of your car unless you feel comfortable. Always let a friend or family member know where and when you are meeting someone.

2. Always be aware of who is around you. Before you get out of a car or turn a corner, make yourself aware of who is around. Police report that many attackers use the element of surprise. Do not let yourself be surprised.

3. Do not arrange to meet people to look at an apartment or a house when it is dark. Try to schedule meetings during daylight hours. Check out the neighborhood at various times of the day, especially afternoons and late evenings.

4. Carry mace or some keys in your hand to use for self-defense. Take a self-defense course. It can be fun and it could save your life.

5. Get good directions to where you are going. Repeat them to the person giving them to you to make sure that you will not get lost.

6. Carry a personal alarm. These are loud alarms that you can carry with you and use to attract attention to yourself should a dangerous situation arise.

7. If you must be out and about at night, **try your best to**

park and walk in well-lighted areas.

8. Call the police station. They should be glad to tell you about a neighborhood or area of town if you are not certain about it. Give them the address of where you are going and they probably can tell you if it is a good street or a street with a lot of crime problems.

9. Always keep your car doors locked.

Steps You Can Take to Protect Yourself and Your Loved Ones in your Home

When inspecting a new place to live, check all of these things out. If any are not satisfactory to you, see if your landlord or potential landlord will correct the problems. It will not only protect you, it could protect *them* from a costly lawsuit should something happen. It could also increase the value of their property.

1. Is the place well-lit? Criminals do not like lights, so make sure all parking and walking areas, stairs, entrances and doorways are well-lit. If you are looking at a place during the day, look for lights. Better yet, drive by at night and see for yourself how well-lit the place is. Ask your landlord to install more lights if necessary. They do not cost a lot, they protect you and your landlord's property, and make it more appealing and safe. Everyone but potential criminals will be a winner.

2. Check the locks on all doors and windows. Deadbolts are an excellent idea. Ask your landlord for extra locks, deadbolts, even a security door may be a good idea. Again, try to convince the landlord that it is in their interest also.

3. Check with the Police about the neighborhood.
Do not rely on others to inform you about crime problems. Call the police yourself. You can also talk to neighbors about the crime situation, but always go directly to the source. Ask the police—they should tell you.

4. Look for Overgrown Bushes and Trees. Criminals love hiding places. If the place is overgrown, ask the landlord and/or maintenance service to cut down or trim bushes and trees and make everyone's place safer.

5. Are there Peepholes? You should always know who is at your door. If there are no peepholes, try to have a wide-angle peephole installed in the entrance door to your apartment.

6. Is there an alarm system? If there is not, perhaps you and your landlord or potential landlord could negotiate for one. Again, it can protect you and enhance the value of your landlord's property.

7) Is/are there a doorman, security guard or company, gate, pass keys to elevators, surveillance cameras? If you are going to be renting in an apartment complex or condominium, these security measures are very important. See what is provided and perhaps you and other tenants can get together to ask your landlord for some of these security measures if it is reasonable. Have your landlord install a security system. It will help you and increase the value of your landlord's property.

8) Is there a neighborhood watch or similar program? Are the landlord and tenants working together to help keep the neighborhood safe? These programs can be very effective in combatting crime. If your neighborhood doesn't yet have such a program, consider starting one with the help of your local police station.

9) How are the other tenants screened? This may be the most important question regarding your security. If your landlord is not screening the tenants, your neighbors may be the criminals! Many landlords do not do background checks on their tenants. It is fairly easy to do and they should. Make sure that your landlord carries out a thorough background check on all potential renters.

What You Can Do To Help

If you would like to make your neighborhood a safer place, you can do it! Get involved with the National Association of Renter's Rights **Taking Back Our Neighborhoods Program!**

The program is simple. You can take responsibility for your home and get other renters, concerned citizens, the police and your landlord to work together to take back your neighborhood. If you do not want to do it for yourself and your own safety, do it for the children who have to grow up in your neighborhood. Here is what you can do to help.

1. Begin a neighborhood watch. The police will help you start one. Call them now. Work with your neighbors and your landlord to help watch out for each other.

2. If you see someone or something suspicious, contact the police immediately. Call your neighbors and have them call also.

3. If you have a serious crime problem in your area, call, write, and keep calling and writing to your landlord, the police, city council and the mayor's office until something is done about it.

4. Make security a priority by having the landlord:
   • install better lighting

59

- cut overgrown bushes
- make sure all locks work
- install deadbolts
- put in peepholes in entrance doors
- add security alarms and/or a security company
- post no trespassing signs

5. Organize a party to get to know your neighbors. Perhaps you can get your landlord to help you arrange it. Exchange phone numbers with your neighbors and watch out for each other. We are all part of a community.

Leaving Town?

Remember, a deserted house or apartment is an open invitation to criminals. Don't advertise the fact that you are not at home! If you are going to be away from your home for a few days or longer, remember to:

1. Stop your mail or have someone pick it up for you.

2. Stop all newspapers or have someone collect them for you.

3. Leave lights on.

4. Leave a radio on, T.V. on. It probably will not run your electric bill up that much.

5. Let a trusted neighbor know you are gone so that they can watch out for suspicious activity.

Protect Yourself

You may not realize it, but if you are a renter, you need renters' insurance. Your landlord's insurance generally does **not** cover your personal belongings. If there were a fire, theft, or water damage, you could possibly lose everything—your clothes, jewelry, T.V., furniture, and stereo equipment. Unfortunately, this happens to thousands of people every year. Even if your landlord were to blame for the loss or damage, it could take a long time to collect from them. You might have to hire an attorney, and wait months or perhaps years to get any compensation. Even then, it is possible that you might not get anything at all.

Please consider reviewing and purchasing renters' insurance. It can be very affordable. Depending on your particular situation, location and needs, it could cost as little as $18 a month for $20,000 of coverage. A small payment each month could buy you great peace of mind.

SMOKE ALARMS

Please help save a life — your own life or the life of someone you love. Make sure your apartment has at least one functioning smoke alarm for every level of your place. Check and test each smoke alarm every month. Do it when you pay the rent. Make sure that you have plenty of working smoke detectors. Never move into a place until the smoke detectors are in place.

8

Getting Repairs Done

Ideally, your landlord should make sure that any repairs you request are completed within a few days of your first request. If, however, you cannot get your landlord to make repairs or comply with some other clause of your lease, you *can* take action. In many states it is possible to deduct the cost of the repairs from your next rent payment or you may even be able to withhold your rent payment until the repairs are made. Of course, you must be sure that deducting repair costs or withholding rent money is legal in your state before you do it. Consult an attorney and check the Appendix at the back of this report before you send one of these letters to your landlord.

Requesting Repairs

To: Landlord's Name
From: Tenant's Name

Date:
RE: Repair Request, your address

Dear (Landlord's Name):

I have been living at the above address since (date). Since that time, I have discovered various defects in the rental unit requiring attention.

The needed repairs are:
1. (example: broken air conditioning unit)
2. (example: garbage in back yard)
3. (example: sink backs up)
4. (example: screens torn or missing)

I hope you will take quick action to remedy these problems. Thank you for your consideration.

Sincerely, (Your Name)

Repair and Deduct: Notification

Before sending a Repair and Deduct notification, you should make sure that your state allows for repair and deduct remedies. See the Appendix or consult an attorney for further details.

To: Landlord's Name
From: Tenant's Name
Date:
RE: Repair and Deduct Notice, your address

Dear (Landlord's Name):

In my letter dated (date of first letter), I notified you of the need for repairs at (your address). It has been _____ days since I wrote, and these repairs have not yet been made.

According to our state's law, I am entitled to "repair and deduct" if I give you reasonable written notice. I feel that I have been more than reasonable in this case.

I am enclosing copies of three (3) estimates for the repairs listed in my previous letter. Unless I hear from you within _____ hours, I am going to hire (name of company, the lowest bidder) to make these repairs.

(If you are withholding rent) I will pay the company myself using rent money previously withheld.

(If you are deducting rent) I will pay the company myself and deduct the amount from my next rent.

Once available, copies of receipts will be sent to you.

Sincerely,
(Your Name)

Withholding Rent

Before withholding rent, make sure that it is allowed in your state.

To: Landlord's Name
From: Tenant's Name
Date:
RE: Repair Request, your address

Dear (Landlord's Name):

In my letter dated (date of your first letter), I notified you of the need for several repairs at the above address. Since you have chosen not to respond to my letter or take steps to remedy the problems, it is necessary for me to take further action.

I have opened a savings account. Until the repairs are completed to my satisfaction I will be depositing my rent money into this account instead of giving it to you. If you wish to discuss my rent withholding or your failure to carry out repairs, please feel free to contact me.

I hope that this problem can be resolved to our mutual satisfaction.

Sincerely,
(Your Name)

WHAT ELSE YOU CAN DO

Remember, every renter receives a warranty with their place. According to laws in just about every state, you deserve a clean, safe, and functioning place in which to live. If repairs are not done within a "reasonable" amount of time, your landlord may be violating the "warranty of habitability", be breaking your lease and is probably violating a local health or building/housing code.

Let your landlord know, after you have given them ample notice, that you may have to contact the local health and/or building codes department. Please do this only after your landlord has not made the repairs. Please realize that this will probably really upset your landlord. A city inspector may come out and demand that your landlord make the necessary repairs within a certain amount of time. If the repairs are not done, then the landlord may be fined by the city.

Also, be aware that if your place is really unsafe, the city may condemn it and require that you move. You probably should consult an attorney to inquire about help with your moving costs.

Remember, if you are having bad repair problems, it may be

best to consider relocating. Negotiate with your landlord to get your deposit back, a concession on rent, if possible, and be sure to screen your next landlord so that hopefully, you will not have these types of problems even again.

9

What To Do If You Can't Pay the Rent

Almost everyone, at some time or another, will have troubles paying their bills. How many times have you read or heard about some multi-millionaire who at one time was broke and had to wash dishes in order to eat or who was evicted?

If you are having trouble paying your bills, especially the rent, you are not alone. There is hope. The real problem is that many people are unwilling to take action to help themselves solve their problem. They would much rather try to ignore it. Do not stick your head in the sand like this! Ask your landlord for advice and help. Seek support from your family, friends, and people you respect and trust. Talk to people you know who are smart financially. Help is out there. You just need to help yourself to find that help.

Nothing is guaranteed in life, but if you will really try some of the following recommendations, you may be able to solve your problems.

1. Take Charge. You have a choice. You could ignore the situation until your landlord and creditors contact you about it. This is not the smart choice. By this time, you can be sure that they are on the offensive because they have been inconvenienced. If they have to contact you first about unpaid rent and bills, they may also trust you less. Many people say "the best defense is an offense!" If you take charge of the situation, the landlord may be more willing to listen to you, trust you, and work with you. Come clean, and do it now. Explain your situation and detail what you plan to do about it. There is help designing your plan of action later in this section.

2. Review all of your Sources for Borrowing the Cash that you Need. Review all of your sources for borrowing money. Perhaps you have available credit through your bank, credit union, employer savings program, credit cards, car title loan companies, life insurance policy, savings and loan association, brokerage accounts, or signature loan offices. But remember, only borrow money you can really pay back. You do not want to make your situation any worse.

3. Check Out Local Governmental Agencies. Many cities have agencies that could possibly help you with your late rent payment. Many such agencies will grant you or loan you money to help you avoid eviction. You may need to make a number of phone calls before you locate an agency that can help you, but they do exist in many places. See the list of agencies in your state located in the appendix for help in starting to locate this kind of help in your community.

4. Contact Churches, Synagogues, United Way Agencies, Big Brother and other charities. Though it may not seem appealing to you to ask for help from a religious institution or charity, many of them are there for just that. Many people at some point in their lives have had to ask for help. Jesus was reportedly born in a manger because his parents could not find or afford a place to sleep. The Jews were homeless for over 40 years and wandered in a desert after leaving Egypt. Many other great religious leaders and founders have been homeless. These institutions and charities are dedicated to helping people in need. If you are not able to pay the rent, you may be eligible for their assistance. Help yourself by letting others help you. One renter who got way behind on the rent raised over $1,200 in a few days from the types of charities discussed here. She was able to avoid eviction. Now she is active in one of the charities that helped her.

5. Face Reality. Most renters will not admit to themselves that they cannot pay the rent or are getting dangerously behind. Assess your situation, be realistic and try not to stress yourself out. Spend your time and energy not on worrying about your problems, but on solving them.

6. Start Talking to your Landlord Now. Don't wait until the rent is late. Most tenants never let their landlords know about their inability to pay the rent on time or pay the rent at all. The only way the landlord finds out about the problem is by discovering that the rent is late. At this point, the landlord is already upset. More time passes as late notices are sent and then eviction may begin. Good communication can help. Communicate with your landlord. Many landlords will understand your problem and be willing to work with you. Most do not want a vacant rental unit, nor do they really want to evict anyone because they generally lose a lot of money and it is a big headache. So, tell your landlord about your situation now instead of later, and:

7. Try to Negotiate a Payment Plan. Your landlord just wants the money. They would prefer to have it when it's due, but generally they would much rather take it later than never. Call your landlord and explain your situation calmly. Be polite and be brief. No one wants to hear a long, drawn-out set of excuses, however good they may be. Instead, quickly offer a realistic payment plan that you can carry out. Do not just tell your landlord what he wants to hear. And don't commit yourself to a payment plan that you cannot afford. You are already going to be late once, do not do it twice. Your credibility with your landlord would be completely ruined.

Be prepared for some resistance to your payment plan or even to your news that you will be late with the rent. However, with some patience and persistence you have a pretty good chance of working something out with your landlord. Always be polite and try to stay calm when working with your landlord.

8. If You Do Make an Agreement, Put it in Writing. The best way is to put your payment plan agreement in writing and have it signed by both your landlord and yourself. If it is really inconvenient to have your landlord sign the agreement, you should at the very least write down your agreement in simple language. Use the words you would use to tell a friend about it. Don't try to sound like a lawyer. The best agreements are simple and could be understood by a 12-year-old. Send a copy of your agreement to your landlord and keep a copy for yourself. Be sure to sign and date it.

Example:

Dear Landlord,

As we talked about and agreed last night, I will send you $100 this week, $100 next week, and the rest of my rent by the 20th of the month. Thank you for allowing *me to do this.*

Your Name
June 4, 1996

9. Rent is a Priority. If you are behind on your rent, you are probably having problems with your other bills, too. However, you must prioritize your bills as to the importance of each one. Generally, paying your rent so that you have a place to live is more important than an expensive stereo system. Try to work out solutions with your other creditors also. Use some of the strategies listed in this chapter to deal with them. If you are being bothered by creditors, learn your rights. You may want to call a local credit counseling firm for further advice.

10. Find Ways to Raise Cash to Pay Your Rent and Bills
Almost everyone can raise some cash if they have to. What many people do instead, however, is become upset, depressed, or just avoid thinking about an unpleasant financial situation. You can be different. Here are just a few ways you might be able to raise some extra cash to help pay the rent:

- **Sell something.** Most people are so attached to their stuff that they would not even dare think about selling any of it. Perhaps you have an extra car, some collectibles, T.V.s, stereos, jewelry, some investments. You must set your priorities. A place to live should be more important than your favorite T.V. set.

- **Get an extra job.** As unpleasant as it may be to work even harder than you already are, you could consider getting an extra job. Work part-time for a while to try and get ahead on your bills.

- **Get an advance from your employer.** Ask your boss for an advance on your pay. Please be careful. Do not ask if you suspect the request would make your boss very uncomfortable. You do not want to risk losing your job. If your employer *is* willing to help, take care not to get such a large advance that your next paycheck is too small to cover the next month's bills.

- **Exchange your Services for the late Rent.** As you learned earlier, you can clean, paint, babysit, do book keeping or any number of services for your landlord in exchange for a discount on your rent or to make up for late or unpaid rent. Everyone has a skill. Use yours. Be careful to negotiate a good fair amount of pay for your work and, as always, get it in writing.

- **Get Help from Family and Friends.** As difficult as it may be for you, you may want to turn to your family and friends for help. Even though this may be awkward for you and your family member or friend, it will probably be less painful and embarrassing than being evicted. You probably know someone with some extra money. Talk to them. See if they can help you and work out a comfortable plan to pay them back. Even though they may be close to you, put it in writing, so that you can both feel comfortable that there will be no disagreement about your agreement.

- **Cut Your Expenses.** Review all of your bills and cut any and all expenses you can. So many renters are evicted—yes, put out on the street!— for not having paid their rent, but their deluxe cable bill is paid, as is the payment on their luxury automobile, expensive stereo system, and 19-feature phone system. Review all of your bills and expenses and see if you can cut any of them. Not paying your rent can have drastic consequences. This may be a time for some drastic expense cutting.

Take Action

Take five minutes right now to review your situation and this information. Replace your worry with a written plan. It will help you greatly when you talk with your landlord and others about finding solutions to your financial problems.

Example:

My Action Plan
Rob Renter, 100 Jones St., #201, Rentland, Ohio
January 2, 1996

I am unable to pay my $425 rent now. I plan to:

- *Call my landlord today and offer to pay him $100 today, $100 next week and the balance by the 28th of the month.*
- *Talk to my employer about a $100 advance*
- *Borrow $100 from my credit cards (I have prioritized my expenses and borrowing sources)*
- *Cut my cable off*
- *Sell my stereo*
- *Try to sell my car and get a less expensive one*
- *Get an extra part-time job to pay off some debt.*

If you are struggling to pay your rent, make your plan today! Put debts and deadlines on your plan and stick to it. Try to read a book or take a course about getting out of debt and budgeting. Good luck, and remember, you have already taken a positive step by reading this information. Keep up the good work!

10

Breaking Your Lease

If you know that you are only going to live somewhere for a short time, perhaps only three to five months, then you may not need a lease. Think carefully before you decide to do without a lease, however. It is still probably better to have all agreements in writing, including your rental terms so that confusion is kept to a minimum. Remember that if you do not have a lease, you can be asked to move or have your rent raised, usually with no more than 30 days notice. If you pay your rent weekly, then your landlord could perhaps raise your rent or give you notice to move in just one week. Imagine how difficult it might be to have to come up with extra rent money or to find a new place in just seven days.

If you do have a lease and have already signed it, but you have to move out before your lease is over, you need to read on. Generally, if you break a lease, you can be held accountable for the remaining months left on your lease and more than likely, you will lose your security deposit. Your main worries are probably having your credit marked and/or wrecked by your landlord, being sued for the thousands of dollars of rent you may owe, never being able to rent a new place because you cannot get a referral from your landlord, and having to remain somewhere you do not want to be. Don't worry! There are some preventive measures you can take and some solutions to make sure that breaking your lease doesn't break you.

Before signing a lease, you can negotiate for and agree to an exit clause for yourself. You can put into the lease that "if you are transferred, buy a house, have to relocate..." you can be let out of your lease, with 30 or 60 days notice. You could offer to forfeit your security deposit and/or one half a month's rent. Remember to be a good negotiator and put all agreements in writing.

If you are already into a written lease and want to or have to break it, you need to know the following:

1. Your lease is a contract. If it is for 12 months at $400 per month, then you owe your landlord $4800. If you leave after 6 months, you technically still owe your landlord $2400. However,

2. Your landlord has a duty to mitigate or lessen their damage. This means that they must and should try to rent out the property after you are gone to reduce the amount you owe them. For instance, if you have a 12-month lease and you leave after 6 months, the landlord should not wait for the remaining 6 months of the lease to elapse before attempting to rent out the property again. They must make an effort to find a new tenant to take over the rent payments. If they rent the property one month after you are gone, then, technically, you would only owe one months' rent, plus whatever security deposit you lost, plus any damages for which you were held responsible.

By knowing your rights and your landlord's responsibilities, you can avoid having to pay the entire year's rent if you must break your lease. Remember too that to be able to get any money from you, the landlord will have to sue you and prove that they could not rent the property for all of the months that you had left on your lease. If may be difficult for them to prove that this was the case. Nevertheless, you should not enter into any agreement, contract, or lease that you cannot keep. However, if unforeseen circumstances do occur, and they often do in life, try to do the right thing

Many renters know that they will have to break a lease, and when the time comes, they do so by packing and leaving in the middle of the night. The landlord finds out about it from the neighbors, the repair person, or worse still, after the next month's rent is past due. The result is an angry landlord, and angry landlords like to vent their anger by suing. Very often, people sue only when they are really hurt or really angry. If you try to never hurt anyone or make them really angry, then your chances of being sued are greatly diminished. So, if you are not finished with your lease but you have to move and break your lease, what can you do?

The Right Thing

Now that you know more about the rules of breaking the lease, you are in a better position to negotiate and do the right thing. If you have to or need to move, you should give your landlord as much notice as possible. Do it politely and in writing. Before you move out, you can offer to help your landlord rent out your apartment. Remember, the sooner the apartment is rented, the less you will owe the landlord. You can help your landlord rent the place by:

1. Getting the word out that your place will be available. Tell friends and colleagues, hand out flyers, etc. If the reason you are moving is because your landlord is really bad, you may not want to do this!

2. Making it easy for your landlord to show your place. Tell your landlord in writing that since you must break your

lease, you will do everything possible to make it easy for your landlord to rent it. Offer to have an open house, help pay for an ad in the newspaper (often they cost no more than $35-60, much less than 3 months' rent).

Why offer to do these things/ Because not only is it the right thing to do, but it is the smart thing to do. Remember you could be held responsible for paying all off the remaining months on your lease, but your landlord generally has a duty to mitigate or lessen his damages by re-renting your place.

If you give the landlord 60-90 days notice and help them rent out the place by about the time you leave, you may save yourself a lawsuit and/or hundreds, if not thousands of dollars. If you offer to do these things and the landlord is angry anyway and still sues you, you will still probably be better off. If you do have to go to court and you have copies of the written offers you made to the landlord to help him rent your place out, your case will probably look better to the judge. And, if you can prove that you offered to help the landlord find a new tenant, the judge may be less likely to award the landlord all of the rent you could not pay. Do the right thing, document it, and you will probably be better off.

Finding a Replacement — Sub-Leasing

If you must break your lease, you can try to find a replacement who can move into your place and hopefully get you out of your lease. This is called sub-leasing. Before you do it, you should check your lease. If it says that sub-leasing is not allowed, the you must get your landlord's permission in writing. The best way to do this is to modify your lease. Get your landlord to agree to it, then scratch out the "no sub-leasing" part of your lease and have your landlord and yourself sign it and date it.

The Rules of Sub-Leasing

1. If your lease prohibits it, you can not do it.

2. If it does, you and your landlord must modify it in writing.

3. Then you must find someone to sublet!

4. You will still be liable for the rent and damage if the person you sublet to does not pay the rent or causes damage.

5. The landlord will come after you for the money and then you will have to go after the person you got to sub-lease.

6. Make sure you and whomever you have sub-leasing have a lease in writing.

7. Before you sub-lease, make sure that the person to whom you are sub-leasing is trustworthy. Run a credit check (you can look in the Yellow Pages and arrange to have this done.) Check with their employer and two previous landlords. Have them fill out an application and agree to the credit check and background check in writing. If you don't, you may be sorry!

A Better Way

Sub-leasing is like becoming a landlord. You must screen your new sub-lessee or tenant and make sure that they pay on time and take care of your place.

This is a lot of responsibility and more often than not, problems occur. What is worse is that many times people sublet to their friends. After one or two months of late payments, problems with repairs and responsibilities, etc., they are not only out of some money, but they may also lose a friend. Perhaps a better way to break your lease is to

1. Inform your landlord.

2. Negotiate with your landlord.

3. Find someone to step into your lease.

4. Get that person and your landlord to sign an agreement.

5. Have your landlord release you from your lease.

When you first ask your landlord to break the lease, expect that they are going to be upset and refuse. What you need to do is inform, educate, and negotiate. Tell the landlord that you want to help them out and be fair. Also, tell them that you want to work it out so that the landlord will get what they want — no headaches, the rent, and the property taken care of. If they are willing to work with you, you will help them find a great new tenant, the rent will not be interrupted, and there will be no costly move in and move out expenses. The landlord may even already know of someone who is looking for a place.

What are the benefits to the landlord for letting you break your lease and allowing someone else to move in? You can explain to the landlord that by working with you, they can avoid a lot of stress and hassle. Add that if you cannot agree to work together and you have to break your lease, the landlord may have to sue you for the rest of the lease. Remind the landlord they might have to hire an attorney, go to court, get a judgment and then go to collect the money if they win. The law in most states says that the landlord has to make a reasonable effort in any case to re-rent the apartment if you break your lease. By renting out the property sooner rather than later, the landlord will save time and money. If the landlord rents it out 2 months after your departure, they can only charge you for the two months the apartment was vacant, not the 6 months remaining on your lease when you left. However, if you help the landlord find a new tenant before you leave, they will get all six months' rent and they won't have to go to the trouble of collecting the money from you.

As for you, the renter, your credit could be damaged. Your landlord might get a judgment against you and you might have to pay a lot of money. It is in your interest to work it out, too. Help the landlord rent your unit before you have to leave. Clean the apartment and make it look like it did when you moved in and negotiate with your landlord. Breaking a lease does not always have to be a lose-lose situation. Work with your landlord. Inform them about how it could be a win-win situation. It is the better way.

If your landlord will not cooperate, try to rent the property for them. Get the landlord's permission to sublease if it is prohibited in your lease. Document that people wanted to rent your apartment but the landlord would not cooperate. Use photos and a move in/move out inspection sheet to show that you left your place in great shape. If you do have to go to court, speak to a local attorney and take your documentation with you.

What If Your Landlord Breaks the Lease?

That's right! Renters are not the only ones to break a lease; landlords often do. Your landlord can break a lease in many ways. Here are some of them:

1. Implied in almost all leases is what is called the warranty of habitability. You probably did not know that your place came with a warranty, but rest assured that it does, and this means that the landlord has to give you a place that is livable. In most instances, this means that it has to be clean, be acceptable by health and safety standards and codes in your area, and that everything is safe and it works. This generally includes plumbing that functions, heat that works, doors and windows that open and close properly, and of course, the place should be free of bugs and rodents.

If the rental unit is lacking and is not really livable for an unreasonable amount of time — more than 30 days would probably be considered unreasonable, although you may feel that more than 12 hours is quite unreasonable — then the landlord may be breaking your lease and violating local health and safety codes.

2. If your place is in a dangerous area and your landlord is not trying to help keep your place safe, your landlord may be breaking the lease. Your landlord can not be held responsible for the whole neighborhood, but if your landlord controls your building and/or your neighbors' building(s) and those neighbors pose a threat to you and your family's safety, your lease may be broken. Notify your landlord and the place in writing if there are dangerous people or activities in your area. If nothing is done about it and a person would feel reasonably unsafe and the landlord is to blame, you probably have a good argument for leaving, with notice, because you do not have a habitable place to live. Check with a local attorney before you move to make sure you can do this and that your landlord really is breaking the lease.

3. If your landlord is not fulfilling any or all of the written lease or rental agreements currently in place, then the landlord is probably breaking the lease. If, for instance, your lease calls for the landlord to pay the utilities and they are not paid for, then your lease may be broken. If the landlord is supposed to supply you with appliances, but has not done so, your lease may also be broken. Read your lease very carefully and understand exactly what your and your landlord's responsibilities are.

If your lease is broken by the landlord, read your lease to find out what your remedies are. Notify the landlord right now if they are breaking the lease. Do it politely and do it in writing. Don't forget to keep a copy. If the landlord continues to break the lease, you may be able to sue for damages, deduct part of your rent into an escrow account until the problem is fixed. If the problem continues and your living conditions are unbearable, you could move out. Realize that the landlord may come after you legally, so be sure to have your situation well-documented so that you can defend yourself if necessary.

Bear in mind, however, that most landlord-tenant problems can be worked out if proper communication is established. Let your landlord know if you are having problems. Be persistent and stand up for your rights. If people are willing to work together, almost any problem can be solved.

11

Going From Renting To Home Ownership

Why should you become a homeowner?

	Renter Average Apartment	Homeowner $65,000 house
Monthly payment	$550	30 yr, 8% interest ____
Appreciation	0	3%/year or $____/year
Equity after 30 years		
	spent at least $550 x 360 (rent usually goes up)	$65,000 or value of house which could be higher (house payment is fixed)

Tax savings	0	Can deduct interest part of payment which in year could be $5,000
Equity Build-up	0	Part of each payment reduces the debt ___
Pride	?	It is yours. If you improve it, you get the benefit.

After one year of renting at $550, you will have almost nothing to show for it. You will have rented for one years. If you buy a house at the end of one year, you will have earned a $5,000 tax write-off for mortgage interest paid, enjoyed some appreciation (perhaps 3% x a $65,000 house = $1,950), paid off some of the debt on your house, and have pride of ownership. Let's say you get a 15-year mortgage. In 15 years, you will have a $65,000 house paid off. No more mortgage or rent payments. Also, if the home appreciates or goes up in value, it might be worth $80,000 or even $120,000. If you rent for 15 years at $550 per month, you will have spent $99,000, and you will own nothing. Of course, if your rent increases over those fifteen years, more than likely, you will have spent over $100,000.

Now, besides going to the bank and trying to buy a house outright, it is time to show you another way you can get some of the benefits of ownership, stop throwing all of your rent away and not have to burden yourself with getting a big loan.

Lease with an Option to Buy

As a renter, you have or will have a least. What you want to try to get is an option to buy. This may not work very well if you are in an apartment complex. It could work if you are renting or thinking about renting a house, condo, or perhaps a duplex. However, once you learn about a lease-option, you may want to find a landlord who will lease-option a house to you.

What is an Option?

An option gives you the right to buy something, in this case a house or condo for a set price. The option price is good for as long as you make the option good. If you have an exclusive option to buy, the seller cannot sell the property to anyone but you for as long as the option is valid. Also, you do not have to buy the house if you do not want to — you have the option to buy.

Perhaps you are thinking that you would not ever want to buy the house or condo that you are renting or considering renting. That does not matter, because by using options you can
1) Stop throwing all of your rent away with nothing to show for it.

2) Maybe make hundreds or thousands of dollars by understanding and using options regardless of whether you want to live in the place for the rest of your life or not.

Warning: Options will not work on apartment units. You must have a place that has a separate legal description, such as house or condominium.

Have you ever rented a house or condo and watched as prices go up? Who benefits? The landlord or whoever the owner is. If you get an option to buy the property at a set price, you could be the one to benefit if the property goes up in value. It is fairly simple. Here is how it can work for you: If you are interested in a house or condo, negotiate the best rent possible as you would anyway. Ask the landlord if they are the owner, because you may be interested in purchasing the property. You must have the owner, whoever it may be, to agree to the option, because the only person who can sign an option is the person who can sell you the property.

Be careful of this as many times you may be dealing with a property manager and not with the owner.

1) Try to determine the value of the house or condo in today's market
- talk to the neighbors. They may know what houses in that area are selling for.
- call a Realtor and ask them to help you to determine the market value of the house. Tell them that if you sell the house (and read on, you may) you may use them as your real estate agent.
- call on other real estate signs in the area to see what those similar houses in the same area as the home you are looking at are selling for.
- call the property tax office and give them the address of the property you are looking at. They can tell you what the city has valued the property at and who is the owner. They can also give you the owner's address. Also, most real estate agents can look up the information in their computers.

If you are really serious about finding out what a property is really worth, get an appraisal done on the property. Perhaps you could negotiate with the owner to split the cost of the appraisal. However, once you get an appraisal and the owner knows about it, they will probably want to get a fair price or the appraised price for their property.

Basically, you can determine the value of a house or condo with just a few phone calls and some research. If the property needs repairs, you should get a reliable estimate of the repairs and subtract that from the value you have given the property. Get a real contractor to give you a bid on the repairs or at the very least have a friend who is really handy to help you inspect the property and assist you in writing out a list of all the repairs necessary. Go room by room, door knob by door knob. Put it in writing. Materials and labor should be included in your written estimate for repairs.

Value of house $65,000
Needs repairs of $ 3,000
Market value today $62,000

Find out from the Realtors in the area how easily a house like the one you are looking at will sell.

Now, after you have negotiated the best monthly rent possible, you start negotiating for the nest purchase price to buy the house. Remember, you do not have to buy it; I just want to show you a way you can make some money, but of course you can buy it.

Remember when negotiating, let the other party, the owner in this case, speak first. Ask them "what is the best price you could give me so that I might buy this house?" They may say $70,000, which is too high if you think it is worth about $62,000, as in our example. They may surprise you and say $51,000. If you never ask, you will never know.

Always negotiate for more. There is big money at stake for you. If they say $51,000, maybe you could offer $46,000. They, they might lower their offer to $48,000. You then offer to split the difference at $49,500, and with some luck, the seller may agree.

You should negotiate the option for as long as you can. Perhaps you can lock in the price for 1 year, 2 years, 3 years, or even 5 years. If the value of the home or condo increases, you can profit from the increase.

If, after some homework on your good negotiating, you optioned the house for $49,500 for three years and the value of the house goes up to $60,000, you can buy the house yourself within the three-year period for $49,500 and you instantly become $10,5000 wealthier. You bought a house, valued at $60,000 for $49,500. If you had not optioned it and locked in the price, you would have to pay the full market price of $60,000.

You can make money at this. Suppose you had no desire to buy he house or condo, but had optioned it anyway. If the house appreciated, as most real estate does over time, you could sell the house for about $60,000, exercise your option, or pay the original owner their $49,5000 that you negotiated, and pocket the difference, less some closing costs. Realistically, you would keep about $7,500. This could make renting less painful. Remember, this can work on $50,000 condos, $100,000 homes, $280,000 homes, and $500,000 estates. Professional real estate investors have made fortunes using options on land, buildings, and even skyscrapers. You can do the same thing with your rental home. Please be sure to get your option in writing. It would be wise to have a local attorney help you with the paperwork, The paperwork is fairly simple and should not cost a lot. Try it. You will probably like it.

Lease Optioning Made Even Better.
Really stop throwing your
rent money away!

You could, with some effort, negotiate a lease-option on a house or condo where you not only lock in a good price to buy the house, but get credit each month towards a down payment.

Suppose you look at a lot of places to rent and find an owner or landlord who is willing to negotiate. Get a three-year option to buy the house for $70,000, Maybe you think that it is worth $70,000 or $76,000. Hopefully, it will go up in value in three years. Your option price of $70,000 is good for three years. Remember, you are not obligated to buy it; instead, you have the option to buy it. It would be even more ideal to negotiate a better price, but here is the good part.

Let's say that you wanted to or were willing to spend $700/month in rent. Negotiate a clause in your option and your lease that $50, $100, $150, or $200 will go towards your down payment. After all, the biggest hurdle for most people to overcome when buying a house is the accumulation of a down payment. If you negotiate this you will have accumulated a substantial amount of money for your down payment. For instance, $100/month for 12 months = $1200. After two years, you could have $2400. This is much better than paying rent and having nothing to show for it. The owner should put this money into an escrow account for you.

Why Would an Owner Do This?

You would be surprised to find out how many people actually do this. It works. You may have to negotiate with a lot of people before you can do it, but you can. Remember, one of a landlord or owner's biggest headaches is minor repairs — leaky sinks, loose door knobs — that renters call them about. If you are willing and able, you can offer to take care of some of or all of these minor repairs in exchange for a good lease option. Offer the landlord the prospect of no more nit-picky repair calls. Also, if you lease-option a place, it is more like yours. If you are going to keep it, or even sell it, you can feel better about improving the property and fixing it up because you will enjoy the benefits of the improvements.

Do not forget to get all agreements in writing and check with a local mortgage company to make sure that you can get credit towards a down payment for your money. Also, instead of a security deposit, your money could go towards the down payment. However, unlike a security deposit, option money towards a down payment is not returnable if you move out. Furthermore, if you do a lease option and do not buy or close on the house, you will probably lose all of the option and escrowed money. However, you probably would not be much worse off than if you had rented, other than the fact that you may not get a security deposit back and may have to do some minor repairs to the property.

This information is intended to give you an idea of some of the possibilities available to you. Please consult a local attorney and/or real estate agent about the details of lease optioning or buying a house on owners' terms.

Stop Throwing Your Rent Away and Start on the Road to Home Ownership

Guess what you get for your rent each month? Not much. You get the use of a place. Granted, this may be good for some people. When you rent, you supposedly have no worries about repairs as the landlord is supposed to take care of everything. But after you move out, you really have nothing to show for all of the rent you paid. If you live somewhere for 2 years paying $500 a month, you pay $500 x 24 = $12,000. Maybe you will be a renter for 20 years. If you rent for 20 years at an average of $500 a month, you will end up spending $120,000, and what will you have to show for it? Fortunately, you do not have to be a renter forever. This chapter will teach you how you can go from being a renter to a homeowner.

Over 90% of all renters want to become homeowners. Maybe you, like many renters, want to be a homeowner some day, but you are not sure how to go from renting to owning. Perhaps, like most people, you do not know how or do not seem able to save up for a downpayment.

Perhaps you do not want the responsibility of owning or are not really settled yet. Here are some quick ideas that can help you stop throwing rent money away, help you save for a downpayment without any extra burden, and perhaps enjoy some of the benefits of owning a home without the burdens or risks.

1) Go to a Bank or Mortgage Company Now. So many people are afraid to go to a bank or mortgage company because their credit may not be perfect or they think that they could never save up for a large downpayment. Put your fears aside and get your information together:

- fill out a financial statement. That bank will give you one. You should have one anyway so go ahead and fill one out.
- get your tax returns for the last two years together
- make a copy of your last month's bank, savings, brokerage and money market accounts
- find your last two paycheck stubs and last year's W-2.

Now go to the bank or mortgage company. You have nothing to lose except perhaps a small application fee or the $45 you may have to pay for a credit report. Many mortgage companies and banks can tell you if you can buy a house (prequalify you) over the phone. At the very least you will put your fear to rest and know if you can afford a house or not. Also, more than likely, the bank will tell you what to do next to pursue your dream of home ownership.

There are any great programs at the banks and mortgage companies for people whose credit is not perfect, or who do not have a lot of money for a downpayment. Some programs will loan money probably at a higher interest rate to people who declared bankruptcy a year or two ago. Also, many banks and governmental agencies have no or very low downpayment programs with low interest rates

The Renter's Rights Handbook

for first time homebuyers and/or low-moderate income families. Take action today!

12

Getting Your Landlord To Fix It

Probably, the most common complaint renters have against their landlord is "I have called and called and they just won't come to fix..." This can be a real headache for you, it can also be expensive, unhealthy, dangerous, illegal, and just plain wrong for a landlord not to fix your reasonable repair request. With prevention, there is no need for a cure. Before you sign a lease, hand over your money or enter into a 1 year relationship with a landlord, find out what the landlord's repair procedure is. Who does the repairs? How long does the landlord say it will take to fix a leaking sink or a broken pipe? Get the landlord to put this information in writing for you. If they are telling you the truth, they should not mind doing this at all. Talk to current residents or renters and ask them about the landlord's response to repair requests. Always inspect your potential new home thoroughly. Check the plumbing, windows, doors, electricity, appliances (turn them on and make sure they work). Take your time. Inspect everything before you sign. Many repair problems experienced by renters were already there before they moved in.

Unfortunately, most people do not take these precautions before they move in and then they are stuck with the problems. They call and call, but the repairs are never made. The most common repair requests are as follows:

• my sink is leaking;
• my commode keeps running;
• the utility bills are so high because the doors and windows are not sealed right;
• the heat does not work;
• the air conditioning does not work;
• the refrigerator or stove is bad.

What To Do

1. Call the landlord. Be polite and ask them when someone will come.

2. Write down your complaint and write down what the landlord said. Date it, send a copy to the landlord and keep a copy for yourself. Do it now, today! So often people forget to do this or mail the complaint and live to regret it!

3. If a repair person does not come as promised or within a reasonable time, call and document your request and the response. Again, copy it and send a copy to your landlord.

4. If the problem is something that is urgent or dangerous, make the landlord aware of it over the phone and in writing. If it is not repaired and poses a danger, let the landlord know that you do not want to, but may have to let the local health and codes department know about this problem if the repair is not made within 2 business days (or any other specified time limit).

5. If, after two verbal and written requests, the landlord still has not responded, you may want to contact your local codes and health department. Officials may come out and inspect your home and notify the landlord or owner of what needs to be repaired. Very often, the landlord will respond. If not, the owner and/or landlord could be fined by the city if the repairs are not made.

6. Some areas of the country (see the appendix for details) allow a renter to deduct the amount of the necessary repair(s) from the rent and pay for the repair. Make sure that you are in an area where this is allowed. Be sure too that you have:
• given your landlord a reasonable amount of time to fix the problem;
• given your landlord written notice that you are going to deduct and repair;
• obtained at least 2, if not 3 written bids for the repair and given copies to your landlord.

Make certain that you have given your landlord a reasonable amount of time. In some cases, this could be 5-30 days. Document everything and you will probably want to send all correspondence return, receipt requested, so that the landlord cannot say "I never knew that you were going to deduct and repair." Consult your local rules and agencies to see if you can deduct and repair (some rules and helpful contacts are included in the appendix).

Note: If the repair not being made poses a real threat to your health and/or safety, the landlord may have broken your lease. More importantly, life is too precious to put your and your family's health and well-being at risk. If you are in danger, let the landlord know, but please leave.

If the landlord has broken your lease by not making a repair in a reasonable amount of time or will not provide you with a safe place to live, you may be able to move.

The Renter's Rights Handbook

Read your lease to find out what it says about it being broken and the damages to which you might be entitled.

Some Important Tips to Remember about Getting a Repair Done

1. Always leave your name, address, phone number, and a simple and accurate description of the problem for your landlord. Do it over the phone, leave a detailed voice mail message, and follow it up in writing. Often, in the excitement of a leaking pipe we forget to leave essential information.

2. Many leases require that a repair request be made in writing. Be sure to keep a copy.

3. If it is an emergency like smoke, a fire, or a crime being committed, call the police and/or fire department first. Keep emergency numbers by the phone. Call your landlord after you have notified the emergency services.

4. Sometimes, the only way that your landlord will know that your repair has not been made is if you tell them. For instance, the landlord's repair team may assure the landlord that the problem has been fixed when really it has not been. Although most repair people are honest and efficient, some of them may not always tell the truth. Don't wait days or weeks: let the landlord know the status of your repair. Be polite, but be persistent.

5. Even if a repair or maintenance person tells you that they will take care of your repair problem, you should always let the landlord know about your repair request too.

6. Always ask your landlord to commit to a specific date and time by when the repair should be made.

7. Do not be shy. It is the landlord's job to fix things that do not work. Make a list. Send it it. Keep a copy.

8. If you are willing and able to make the repair yourself, make sure that you:
• Let the landlord know.
• Agree in writing as to how you will be compensated.
• Do not work for free unless your consider your landlord a charity case or a non-profit institution.
• Are either paid a fair wage and get the money for materials up front or have the cost deducted from the rent.

If you are in a place where there are many repairs that need to be made and are not being made, you may want to consider some of these negotiating tactics. After you have informed your landlord of the requested repairs and nothing has been done, you can let your landlord know that they may be breaking the lease, violating building codes and health regulations, and that you want to offer the landlord the following courses of action:

1. Make the repair within 5 days.

2. Not make the repairs and have codes on top of them and if it is legal you may withhold rent, put it in escrow with the court or an attorney, and you may also have to leave because of unsafe conditions.

3. Agree to let you get the repairs done (if you are willing and able) and deduct the amount from your rent or reimburse you. You must provide bids and receipts.

4. Negotiate a lower monthly rent, since the place is inadequate, for the remainder of your lease.

    Example:
If you are paying $550, but are not getting all that you

are paying for because some things do not work, negotiate a new rent of $500 per month for the remainder of your lease. This way you can pay have the problems fixed, fix them yourself, or just live with them. This is fair because you are not receiving what you initially bargained for. Make sure you negotiate a large enough yet fair discount. Check your lease to see how to change or modify it. Make sure your landlord signs the new rent amount.

Never threaten your landlord. Only mention codes and the health department as a **last resort** after you have given them time to make a repair. As you know, even if you called a repair person today, it would take a few days to get that person to your house. Let your landlord know that it is for their benefit to make the repairs. A leaking sink might be fixed for $45. If it continues to leak, it could destroy the floor, which might cost $450 or more.

Remember, a landlord has a duty to maintain your premises. You, as a renter, can only be held responsible for damage that you do. You are also not responsible for fair wear and tear or what reasonably happens to a place over time. For instance, the carpet becomes worn over the course of a year of two, the paint dulls, some plumbing may leak or clog. None of this is due to excessive use on your part. You are a customer, and if you are given a defective product (a rental unit that really does not function properly) or bad service (nothing gets repaired after you have let the landlord know about it), you have rights.

Just as you can sue a company that sold you a defective product, you can sue your landlord. This really should be the last resort after you have repeatedly informed the landlord of your problems verbally and in writing without any efforts being made to solve them. Try to work it out, but if you cannot, talk with an attorney. If the landlord is really in the wrong, you could be awarded:

1. A partial or total refund of the rent you paid if the court find that the conditions you had to endure were not fair or adequate.

2. Reimbursement for any property that was ruined or lost because of the landlord's failure to fix the problem. For instance, if the hot water heater was not repaired after you had requested its repair, and it burst, ruining your furniture or your clothes, you might be paid for the value of what you lost.

3. Compensation for injury if you or a family member or guest are hurt because of a defect that the landlord should have fixed.

Going to court will probably require an attorney. You can ask to have your attorney's fees paid by the landlord and this may happen, especially if you win your case.

Retaliation is Illegal

Many renters are scared even to ask for repairs. Certainly, many renters think that if they challenge their landlord or maybe repeatedly request repairs, the landlord will raise the rent or evict them.

This is called retaliation. It is wrong and it is illegal. A landlord cannot evict you just because you are exercising your legal rights. The only reason they can evict you is because:
• you didn't pay the rent;
• you pose a danger to the neighbors;
• you have violated your lease agreement;
• your lease is over.

Retaliation by a landlord is illegal. If you feel you are a victim of this, contact an attorney or your local Attorney General's office (see appendix).

Some Quick Repair Tips

1. If you have a bad plumbing leak, turn the water cut off valve off. Have your landlord or maintenance man show you where they are. This should stop sink, tub, and commode leaks instantly to prevent further damage and high water bills until the landlord can make the necessary repairs.

2. If you think your utility bill is too high, call the utility company and ask them what an average bill should be. They should be able to tell you. Before you move into a place, you should call and ask about the history of bills of what it costs to pay the gas, water, and electric bills. If something is really wrong, let your landlord know. Have the utility company send you copies of what the bill should be and show your landlord. Negotiate to have the landlord reimburse you for the overcharges if it is really due to the landlord not making a repair promptly.

3. Keep an extra key with a trusted friend or family member who lives nearby. One of the most common repair calls is for a lock out. Often, landlords will charge for this. Save yourself some money and headaches by getting an extra key today.

4. When inspecting a place before you move in, ask and look to see if the place is well insulated. Most of the utility expense comes from the air conditioning and the hot water heater. Most heat loss is through the ceiling and roof, windows and doors. Ask your landlord to fix these things if there is a problem. Remind them that it will increase the value of their property and save them money in the long run as renters will stay longer. There will be less turnover for the landlord and you can save alot of money.

Useful Addresses for Renters

State Laws to Protect Renters' Rights

Disclaimer

The purpose of this publication is to give you general information. It is in no way designed or intended to provide legal advice or specific recommendations. Laws and rules change frequently. The accuracy of laws or recommendation can not be guaranteed. Please consult an attorney and/or accountant before acting upon any of this general information.

STATE CONSUMER PROTECTION OFFICES

Alabama
Consumer Assistance
Office of Attorney General
11 South Union St.
Montgomery, AL 36130
(800)392-5658
(334)242-7334
(334)242-7458-fax

Alaska
Office of Attorney General
PO Box K
State Capitol
Juneau, AK 99811-0300
(907)465-3600
(907)465-2075-fax

Arizona
Consumer Information & Complaints
Office of Attorney General
1275 West Washington St.
Phoenix, AZ 85007
(602)542-5763
(800)352-8431
(602)542-4085-fax

Arkansas
Advocacy Division of Attorney General's Office
200 Callett-Prein Bldg.
323 Center St.
Little Rock, AR 72201
(501)682-2007
(800)482-8982
(501)682-8084-fax

California
Dept. of Consumer Affairs
Consumer Assistance Office
400 R St., Room 1040

Sacramento, CA 95814
(916)445-1254
(800)952-5210
(916)324-4298-fax

Colorado
Consumer Protection Unit
Office of Attorney General
1525 Sherman St., 5th Floor
Denver, CO 80203
(303)866-5189
(800)332-2071
(303)866-5691-fax

Connecticut
Dept. of Consumer Protection
165 Capitol Ave.
Hartford, CT 06106
(860)566-2816
(860)566-1531-fax

Delaware
Dept. of Justice
Consumer Protection Unit
Delaware State Bdlg.
820 North French St., 4th Floor
Wilmington, DE 19801
(302)577-3250
(302)577-2610-fax

District of Columbia
Dept. of Consumer & Regulatory Affairs
614 H Street, NW, Room 1120
Washington, DC 20001
(202)727-7170
(202)727-8073-fax

Florida
Division of Consumer Services
Dept. of Agriculture & Consumer Affairs
235 Mayo Building
Tallahassee, FL 32399

The Renter's Rights Handbook
(904)488-2221
(800)435-7352
(904)488-0863-fax

Georgia
Office of Consumer Affairs
Attorney General's Office
40 Capitol Square SW
Atlanta, GA 30334-1300
(404)656-3794
(404)651-9184-fax

Hawaii
Office for Consumer Protection
Dept. of Commerce & Consumer Affairs
828 Fort St., Room 600B
Honolulu, HI 96813
(808)586-2630
(808)586-2640-fax

Idaho
Consumer Protection Division
Office of Attorney General
PO Box 83720
Boise, ID 83720-0010
(208)334-2424
(800)432-3545
(208)334-2530-fax

Illinois
Consumer Protection Division
Office of Attorney General
500 South 2nd St.
Springfield, IL 62706
(217)782-9011
(800)252-8666
(217)785-2511-fax

Indiana
Consumer Protection Division
Office of Attorney General

Indiana Gov't Center South, 5th Floor
402 West Washington
Indianapolis, IN 46204-2270
(317)232-6205
(800)382-5516
(317)232-7979-fax

Iowa
Consumer Protection Division
Office of Attorney General
1300 E. Walnut
Hoover State Office Bldg.
Des Moines, IA 50319
(515)281-5926
(515)281-4209

Kansas
Consumer Protection Division
Office of Attorney General
301 South West 10th
Topeka, KS 66612
(913)296-3751
(800)432-2310
(913)296-6296-fax

Kentucky
Consumer Protection Division
Office of Attorney General
PO Box 2000
Frankfort, KY 40602-2000
(502)573-2200
(800)432-9257

Louisiana
Consumer Protection Section
Office of Attorney General
PO Box 94095
Baton Rouge, LA 70804-9095
(504)342-9638
(504)342-7901-fax

Maine
Office of Consumer Regulation
35 State House Station
Augusta, ME 04333-0035
(207)624-8527
(800)332-8529
(207)624-8690-fax

Maryland
Consumer Protection Division
Office of Attorney General
200 St. Paul Pl.
Baltimore, MD 21202-2022
(410)576-7003
(410)576-7003

Massachusetts
Consumer Protection Division
Dept. of Attorney General
1 Ashburton Place
Boston, MA 02108
(617)727-7755
(617)727-5762-fax

Michigan
Consumer Protection Divison
Office of Attorney General
PO Box 30213
Lansing, MI 48909
(517)335-0855
(517)373-4916-fax

Minnesota
Citizen Assistance Center
Office of Attorney General
1400 NCL Tower
445 Minnesota St.
St. Paul, MN 55101
(612)296-3353
(800)657-3787

Mississippi
Consumer Protection Division
Office of Attorney General
PO Box 22947
Jackson, MS 39225-22947
(601)359-4230
(601)359-3441-fax

Missouri
Consumer Protection Division
Office of Attorney General
PO Box 899
Jefferson City, MO 65102
(573)751-3321
(800)392-8222
(573)751-0774

Montana
Consumer Affairs Unit
Dept. of Commerce
1424 Ninth Ave
Helena, MT 59620
(406)444-3553
(406)444-2903-fax

Nebraska
Consumer Protection Division
Office of Attorney General
2115 State Capitol Bldg.
PO Box 98920
Lincoln, NE 68509-8920
(402)471-2682
(402)471-3297

Nevada
Consumer Affairs Division
State Mail Room Complex
1850 E. Sahara Ave, Ste. 101
Las Vegas, NV 89158
(702)486-7355
(702)486-2758-fax

New Hampshire
Consumer Protection Bureau
Dept. of Justice
33 Capitol St.
Concord, NH 03301
(603)271-3641
(603)271-2110

New Jersey
Division of Community Affairs
124 Halsey St.
Newark, NJ 07102
(201)504-6200
(201)648-3538-fax

New Mexico
Consumer Protection Division
Office of Attorney General
PO Drawer 1508
Santa Fe, NM 87504
(505)827-6910
(800)678-1508
(505)827-5826-fax

New York
Consumer Protection Board
99 Washington Ave.
Albany, NY 12210
(518)474-8583
(518)474-2474-fax

North Carolina
Consumer Protection Section
Office of Attorney General
Dept. of Justice
Po Box 629
Raleigh, NC 27602
(919)733-7741
(919)733-7491

North Dakota
Consumer Protection Division
Office of Attorney General
600 East Blvd.
Bismarck, ND 58505
(701)328-3404
(800)472-2600
(701)328-2226

Ohio
Consumer Protection Division
Office of Attorney General
State Office Tower
30 East Broad Street, 25th Floor
Columbus, OH 43215-3428
(614)466-3376
(800)282-0515
(614)466-5087-fax

Oklahoma
Consumer Affairs Division
Office of Attorney General
112 State Capitol Building
Oklahoma City , OK 73105
(405)521-4274
(405)521-6246-fax

Oregon
Financial Fraud
Dept. of Justice
1162 Court Street, NE
Salem, OR 97310
(503)378-4320
(503)378-3784

Pennsylvania
Bureau of Consumer Protection
Office of Attorney General
Strawberry Square
14th Floor
Harrisburg, PA 17120

The Renter's Rights Handbook
(717)787-9707
(800)441-2555
(717)787-1190-fax

Rhode Island
Consumer Protection Division
Dept. Of Attorney General
72 Pine St.
Providence, RI 02903
(401)274-4400
(401)274-1331-fax

South Carolina
Department of Consumer Affairs
Po Box 5757
Columbia, SC 29250
(803)734-9452
(800)922-1594
(803)734-9365-fax

South Dakota
Division of Consumer Affairs
Office of Attorney General
State Capitol Building
500 East Capitol
Pierre, SD 57501
(605)773-4400
(605)773-4106-fax

Tennessee
Division of Consumer Affairs
Dept. of Commerce & Insurance
500 James Robertson Pkwy
5th Floor
Nashville, TN 37234-0600
(615)741-4737
(800)342-8385
(615)741-4000-fax

Texas
Consumer Protection Division
Office of Attorney General
PO Box 12548
Austin, TX 78711
(512)463-2070
(512)463-2063-fax

Utah
Division of Consumer Protection
Commerce Dept.
PO BOx 45802
Salt Lake City, UT 84145-0802
(801)530-6619
(801)530-6001-fax

Vermont
Consumer Assistance
Office of Attorney General
109 State St.
Montpelier, VT 05609
(802)656-3183
(800)649-2424
(802)828-2154-fax

Virginia
Office of Consumer Affairs
Dept. of Agriculture & Consumer Services
1100 Bank St.
Richmond, VA 23219
(804)786-2042
(800)552-9963
(804)371-2945

Washington
Consumer Resource Center
Office of Attorney General
PO Box 40100
Olympia, WA 98504
(360)753-6200
(800)551-4636

111

The Renter's Rights Handbook
(360)664-0228-fax

West Virginia
Consumer Protection Division
Office of Attorney General
1800 Quarrier St.
Charleston, WV 25301
(304)558-8986
(800)368-8808
(304)558-0140

Wisconsin
Consumer Protection Agency
Dept. of Justice
123 West Washington Ave.
Room 150
Madison, WI 53707
(608)224-4953
(608)267-2223

Wyoming
Consumer Affairs Division
Office of Attorney General
123 State Capitol Bdlg.
Cheyenne, WY 82002
(307)777-7891
(307)777-6869-fax

STATE AGENCIES FOR FAIR HOUSING

Alaska
Commission on Human Rights
800 A St., Ste. 204
Washington, DC 20009
(907)274-4692

Arizona
Commission on Human Relations
1275 W. Washington St.
Phoenix, AZ 85007
(602)542-5263

Arkansas
Dept. of Housing and Urban Development
TCBY Tower
425 West Capitol Ave., Ste.900
Little Rock, AR 72201
(501)324-6296

California
Dept. of Fair Employment and Housing
1330 Broadway, Ste. 1336
Oakland, CA 94612-2512
(800)233-3212

Colorado
Civil Rights
60 Broadway, Ste. 1050
Denver, CO 80202
(303)894-2997

Connecticut
Commission on Human Rights
90 Washington St.
Hartford, CT 06115
(203)566-4895

Delaware
Division of Human Relations
820 N. French St.

Wilmington, DE 19801
(302)577-3485

District Of Columbia
Commission on Human RIghts
2000 14th St. NW
Washington, DC 20009
(202)939-8740

Florida
Commission on Human Relations
325 John Knox Rd.
Bldg. F, Ste. #240
Tallahassee, FL 32303
(904)488-7082

Georgia
Fair Housing Commission
75 Spring St.
Atlanta, GA 30303-3388
(404)331-3356

Hawaii
Civil Rights Commission
888 Mililani St., 2nd Floor
Honolulu, HI 96813
(808)586-8636

Idaho
Commission on Human Rights
PO Box 83720
Boise, ID 83720
(208)334-2873

Illinois
Dept. of Human Rights
100 West Randolph St., Ste.#10-100
Chicago, IL 60601
(312)814-6269

Indiana
Civil Rights Commission

100 North Senate Ave., Room N103
Indianapolis, IN 46204
(317)232-2600

Iowa
Civil Rights Commission
211 East Maple
Des Moines, IA 50319
(800)457-4416

Kansas
No fair housing organization,
inquiries handled through HUD.

Kentucky
Commission on Human Rights
Heyburn Bldg.
332 W. Broadway, 7th Flr.
Louisville, KY 40202
(502)595-4024

Louisiana
Attorney General, Dept. of Public Protection
PO Box 94095
Baton Rouge, LA 70804-9095
(504)342-9764

Maine
Human Rights Commission
51 State House Station
Augusta, ME 04333
(207)624-6050

Maryland
Commission on Human Relations
6 St. Paul St., 9th Flr., Ste. 900
(410)767-8600

Massachusetts
Commission Against Discrimination
One Ashburton Place
Boston, MA 02108
(617)727-3990

Michigan
Dept. of Civil Rights
State of Michigan Plaza Bldg.
1200 6th St.
Detroit, MI 48226
(313)256-2663

Minnesota
Dept. of Human Rights
500 Bremer Tower
Seventh & Minnesota St.
St. Paul, MN 55101
(612)296-5663

Mississippi
No fair housing organization,
inquiries handled through HUD.

Missouri
Commission for Human Rights
3315 West Truman
Jefferson City, MO 65102
(573)751-3325

Montana
Human Rights Commission
616 Helena Ave.
Helena, MT 59624
(406)444-2884

Nebraska
Equal Opportunity Commission
PO Box 94934
Lincoln, NE 68509
(402)471-2024

Nevada
No fair housing organization,
inquiries handled through HUD.

New Hampshire
Commission for Human Rights
163 Loudon Rd.
Concord, NH 03301
(603)271-2767

New Jersey
Division on Civil Rights
383 West State St.
Trenton, NJ 08625
(609)292-4605

New Mexico
Human Rights Commission
1596 Pacheco St.
Santa Fe, NM 87505
(505)827-6838

New York
Division of Human Rights
55 West 125th St., 13th Flr.
New York, NY 10027
(212)961-8400

North Carolina
Human Relations Commission
217 West Jones St.
Raleigh, NC 27603
(919)733-7996

North Dakota
No fair housing agency,
inquiries handled through HUD.

Ohio
Civil Rights Commission
220 Parsons Ave.
Columbus, OH 43215
(614)466-2785

Oklahoma
Human Rights Commission
2101 N. Lincoln Blvd. #480
Oklahoma City. OK 73105
(405)521-3441

Oregon
Civil Rights Div., Bureau of Labor & Industry
800 NE Oregon St.
Portland, OR 97232
(503)731-4075

Pennsylvania
Human Relations Commission
2971 East North 7th St.
Harrisburg, PA 17110
(717)787-4410

Rhode Island
Commission for Human Rights
10 Abbott Park Pl.
Providence, RI 02903
(401)277-2661

South Carolina
Human Affairs Commission, Fair Housing Div.
2611 Forest Dr., Ste. 200
Columbia, SC 29204
(803)253-6336

South Dakota
Division of Human Rights
222 East Capitol St.
Pierre, SD 57501
(605)773-4493

Tennessee
Human Rights Commission
530 Church St.
Nashville, TN 37243
(615)741-5825

Texas
Commission on Human Rights
6330 Hwy 290E
Austin, TX 78723
(512)437-3450

Utah
Industrial Comm., Anti-Discrimination Div.
160 E. 300 South, 3rd Floor
PO Box 146640
Salt Lake City, UT 84114
(801)530-6801

Vermont
Human Rights Commission
135 State St.
2nd Floor
Mt. Pelier, VT 05633-6301
(802)828-2480

Virginia
Office of Fair Housing
3600 West Broad St.
Richmond, VA 23230
(804)367-8530

Washington
Human Rights Commission
Ste 402 P.O. Box 42490
711 South Capitol Way
Olympia, WA 98504-9024
(360)753-6770

West Virginia
Human Rights Commission
115 Lee St West
Charleston, WV 25302
(304) 308-6880

Wisconsin
Dept. of Industry, Labor and Human Relation

The Renter's Rights Handbook

Equal Rights Division
P.O. Box 8928
201 E. Washington Ave.
Madison, WI 53708
(608)266-7552

Wyoming
No state agency. Contact HUD

HUD OFFICES

REGION 1 (CT, ME, MA, NH,RI,VT)

Boston Regional Office
Thomas P. O'Neill Jr. Fed'l Bldg.
10 Causeway St., Room 375
Boston, MA 02222-1092
(617)565-5234

Field Offices:

Hartford Office
330 Main St., 1st Floor
Hartford, CT 06706
(203)240-4522

Bangor Office
99 Franklin St., 3rd Floor
Bangor, ME 04401-4925
(207)945-0467

Manchester Office
Norris Cotton Fed'l Bldg.
275 Chestnut St.
Manchester, NH 03101-2487
(603)666-7681

Providence Office
10 Weybassett St., 6th Floor
Providence, RI 02903-3234
(401)528-5351

Burlington Office
U.S. Fed'l Bldg.
11 Elmwood Ave. #244
Burlington, VT 05402-0879
(802)951-6290

REGION 2 (NJ, NY)

New York Regional Office
26 Federal Plaza Bldg.
New York, NY 10278-0068
(212)264-6500

Field Offices:

Camden Office
800 Hudson Sq.
Hudson Bldg., 2nd Floor
Camden, NJ 08102-1156
(609)757-5081

Newark Office
One Newark Center, 13th Floor
Newark, NJ 07102-5260
(201)622-7900

Albany Office
52 Corporate Cir.
Albany, NY 12203-5121
(518)464-4200

Buffalo Office
Lafayette Ct.
465 Main St., 5th Floor
Buffalo, NY 14203-1780
(716)551-5755

REGION 3 (DL, DC, MD, PA, VA, WV)

Philadelphia Regional Office
100 Penn Square East
Philadelphia, PA 19107-3390
(215)656-0500

Field Offices:

Wilmington Office
824 Market St., Ste. 850
Wilmington, DE 19801-301
(302)573-6300

Washington D.C. Office
820 1st St.
Union Center Plaza Bldg., 4th Floor
Washington, DC 20002-4205
(202)275-9200

Baltimore Office
City Crescent Bldg.
10 South Howard St., 5th Floor
Baltimore, MD 21201-2505
(410)962-2520

Pittsburgh Office
339 6th St., 6th Floor
Pittsburgh, PA 15222
(412)644-6428

Virginia Office
The 3600 Centre
3600 West Broad St.
Richmond, VA 23230-0331
(804)278-4539

Charleston Office
405 Capitol St., Ste. 708
Charleston, WV 25301-1795
(304)347-7000

Atlanta Regional Office
Richard B. Russell Fed'l Bldg.
75 Spring St. S.W.
Atlanta, GA 30303-3388
(404)331-5136

Field Offices:

Birmingham Office
600 Beacon Pkwy. West, Ste. 300
Birmingham, AL 35209-3144
(205)290-7617

Coral Gables Office
Gables 1 Towers
1320 South Dixie Hwy.
Coral Gables, FL 33146-2911
(305)662-4500

Jacksonville Office
Southern Bell Tower
301 West Bay St.
Jacksonville, FL 32202-5121
(904)232-2626

Miami Office
8600 Northwest 36th St., Ste. 3100
PO Box 4022
Miami, FL 33166-4022
(305)717-2500

Orlando Office
Langley Bldg.
3751 Maguire Blvd., Ste. 270
Orlando, FL 32803-3032
(407)648-6441

Tampa Office
Timberlake Fed'l Bldg. Annex

501 East Polk St., Ste. 700
Tampa, FL 33602-3945
(813)228-2501

Louisville Office
601 West Broadway
PO Box 1044
Louisville, KY 40201-1044
(502)585-5251

Jackson Office
Doctor A.H. McCoy Fed'l Bldg.
100 West Capitol St., Room 910
Jackson, MS 39269-1016
(601)965-5308

Greensboro Office
Koger Building
2306 West Meadowview Rd.
Ste. 2200
Greensboro, NC 27407-3707
(910)547-4000

Caribbean Office
New San Juan Office Bldg.
159 Carlos E. Chardon Ave.
San Juan, PR 00918-1804
(809)766-6121

Columbia Office
Strom Thurmond Federal Bldg.
1835 Assembley St.
Columbia, SC 29201-2480
(803)765-5592

Knoxville Office
John J. Duncan Fed'l Bldg.
710 Locust St., 3rd Floor
Knoxville, TN 37902-2526
(423)549-4389

Memphis Office
One Memphis Place
200 Jefferson Ave., Ste. 1200
Memphis, TN 38103-2335
(901)544-3367

Nashville Office
251 Cumberland Bend Dr., Ste. 200
Nashville, TN 37228-1803
(615)736-5213

REGION 5 (IL, IN, MI, MN, OH, WI)

Chicago Regional Office
Ralph H. Metcalfe Fed'l Bldg.
77 West Jackson Blvd.
Chicago, IL 60604-3507
(312)353-5680

Field Offices:

Springfield Office
509 West Capitol St., Ste. 206
Springfield, IL 62704-1906
(800)206-2379

Indianapolis Office
151 N. Delaware St.
Indianapolis, IN 46204-2526
(317)226-6303

Detroit Office
Patrick V. McNamara Fed'l Bldg.
477 Michigan Ave.
Detroit, MI 48226-4394
(313)226-7900

Flint Office
The Federal Bldg.
605 N. Saginaw, Ste. 200
Flint, MI 48502-2043
(810)766-5108

Grand Rapids Office
Trade Center
50 Louis N.W.
Grand Rapids, MI 48503-3409
(616)456-2100

Minneapolis Office
Henry S. Reuss Fed'l Plaza
220 Second St. South
Minneapolis, MN 55401-2195
(612)370-3000

Cincinnati Office
525 Vine St.
Cincinnati, OH 44202-3188
(513)684-2884

Cleveland Office
Renaissance Bldg.
1350 Euclid Ave., Ste. 500
Cleveland, OH 44115-2499
(216)522-4065

Columbus Office
200 North High St.
Columbus, OH 43215-2499
(614)469-5737

Milwaukee Office
Henry S. Reuss Fed'l Plaza
310 W. Wisconsin Ave., Ste. 1380
Milwaukee, WI 53203-2289
(414)297-3214

The Renter's Rights Handbook
REGION 6 (AR, LA, NM, OK, TX)

Fort Worth Regional Office
1600 Throckmorton
PO Box 2905
Fort Worth, TX 76113-2905
(817)885-5401

Field Offices:

Little Rock Office
TCBY Tower
425 West Capitol Ave., Ste. 900
Little Rock, AR 72201-3488
(501)321-5900

New Orleans Office
Hale Boggs Fed'l Bldg.
501 Magazine St., 9th Floor
New Orleans, LA 70130
(504)589-7200

Shreveport Office
401 Edwards St., Ste. 1510
Shreveport, LA 71101-3107
(318)676-3385

Albuquerque Office
625 Truman St. N.E.
Albuquerque, NM 87110-6443
(505)262-2423

Oklahoma City Office
500 W. Main St., Ste. 400
Oklahoma City, Ok 73102
(405)553-7459

Tulsa Office
50 East 15th St.
Tulsa, OK 74119-4030
(918)581-7434

Dallas Office
Room 860
525 Griffin St.
Dallas, TX 75202-5007
(214)767-8359

Houston Office
Norfolk Tower
2211 Norfolk, Ste. 200
Houston, TX 77098-4095
(713)313-2274

Lubbock Office
George H. Mahon Fed'l Bldg.
1205 Texas Ave.
Lubbock, TX 79401-4093
(806)743-7265

San Antonio Office
Washington Square
800 Doloross St.
San Antonio, TX 78207
(210)229-6800

REGION 7 (IA, KS, MO, NE)

Kansas City Regional Office
Gateway Tower II
400 State St.
Kansas City, KS 66101-2406
(913)551-5462

Field Offices:

Des Moines Office
210 Walnut St.
Des Moines, IA 50309-2155
(515)284-4512

St. Louis Office
Robert A. Young Fed'l Bldg.
1222 Spruce St., Third Floor

The Renter's Rights Handbook
St. Louis, MO 63103-2836
(314)539-6583

Omaha Office
Executive Tower Centre
10909 Mill Valley Rd.
Omaha, NE 68154-3955
(402)492-3100

REGION 8 (CO, MT, ND, SD, UT, WY)

Denver Regional Office
First Interstate Tower North
633 17th St.
Denver, CO 80202-3607
(303)672-5440

Field Offices:

Helena Office
Federal Office Bldg.
Drawer 10095
Helena, MT 59626-0095
(406)449-5205

Fargo Office
653 2nd Ave. Room 366
P.O. 2483
Fargo, ND 58108-2483
(701)239-5136

Sioux Falls Office
2400 West 49th St.
Ste. 1-201
Sioux Falls, SD 57105-6558
(605)330-4223

Salt Lake City Office
257 Tower Bldg.
257 East - 200 South, Ste 550
Salt Lake City, UT 84111-2048
(801)524-5241

Casper Office
Federal Office Bldg.
100 East B St., Room 4229
P.O. Box 120
Casper, WY 82601
(307)261-6250

REGION 9 (AZ, CA, HI, NV)

San Francisco Regional Office
Philip Burton Fed'l Bldg.
450 Golden Gate Ave.
PO Box 36003
San Francisco, CA 94102-3448
(415)556-4752

Field Offices:

Phoenix Office
Two Arizona Center
400 North 5th St., Ste. 1600
Phoenix, AZ 85004-2361
(602)379-4434

Tucson Office
Security Pacific Bank Plaza
33 North Stone Ave., Ste. 700
Tucson, AZ 85701
(602)670-6237

Fresno Office
1630 East Shaw Ave., Ste. 138
Fresno, CA 93710-8193
(209)487-5033

Los Angeles Office
1615 West Olympic Blvd.
Los Angeles, CA 90015-3801
(213)251-7122

Sacramento Office
777 12th St., Ste. 200
Sacramento, CA 95814
(916)498-5220

San Diego Office
Mission City Corporate Center
2365 Northside Dr., Ste. 300
San Diego, CA 92108-2712
(619)557-5310

Santa Ana Office
3 Hutton Centre Dr.
Ste. 500
Santa Ana, CA 92702-5764
(714)957-3741

Honolulu Office
7 Waterfront Plaza
500 Ala Moana Blvd., Ste. 500
Honolulu, HI 96813-4918
(808)522-8175

Las Vegas Office
333 N. Rancho Dr.
Ste. 700
Las Vegas, NV 89119-6516
(702)388-6500

Reno Office
1575 Delucchi Ln.
Ste. 114
Reno, NV 89502-6581
(702)784-5356

REGION 10 (AK, ID, OR, WA)

Seattle Regional Office
Seattle Federal Office Bldg.
909 1st Ave., Ste. 200
Seattle, WA 98104-1000
(206)220-5101

Field Offices:

Anchorage Office
University Plaza Bldg.
949 East 36th Ave., Ste. 401
Anchorage, AK 99508-4399
(907)271-4170

Boise Office
Plaza IV
800 Park Blvd., Ste. 220
Boise, ID 83712-7743
(208)334-1990

Portland Office
400 Southwest Sixth Ave.
Ste. 700
Portland, OR 97204-1596
(503)326-2561

Spokane Office
Farm Credit Bank Bldg.
Eighth Floor East
West 601 First Ave.
Spokane, WA 99204-0317
(509)353-2510

FEDERAL TRADE COMMISSION OFFICES

Atlanta
(AL, FL, GA, MS, NC, SC, TN, VA)
Federal Trade Commision
1718 Peachtree St. N.W.
Rm. 1000
Atlanta, GA 30367
(404) 881-4836

Boston
(CT, ME, MA, NH, RI, VT)
Federal Trade Commission
150 Causeway St. Rm. 1301
Boston, MA 02114
(617) 223-6621

Chicago
(IL, IN, IA, KY, MN, MO, WI)
Federal Trade Commission
55 E. Monroe St., Suite 1437
Chicago, IL 60603
(312) 353-4423

Cleveland
(DE, MD, MI, OH, PA, WV)
Federal Trade Commission
Mall Bldg., Suite 500
118 St. Clair Ave.
Cleveland, Oh 44114
(216) 522-4207

Dallas
(AK, LA, NM, OK, TX)
Federal Trade Commission
8303 Elmbrook Dr.
Dallas, TX 75247
(214) 767-7050

Denver
(CO, KS, MT, NE, ND, SD, UT, WY)
Federal Trade Commission
1405 Curtis St., Suite 2900
Denver, CO 80202
(303) 844-2271

Los Angeles
(AZ, southern CA)
Federal Trade Commission
11000 Wilshire Blvd.
Los Angeles, CA 90024
(213) 824-7575

New York
(NJ, NY)
Federal Trade Commission
Federal Bldg. Rm. 2243-EB
26 Federal Plaza
New York, NY 10278
(212) 264-1207

San Francisco
(northern CA, HI, NV)
Federal Trade Commission
450 Golden Gate Ave. Rm. 12470
San Francisco, CA 94102
(808) 546-5685

Seattle
(AL, ID, OR, WA)
Federal Trade Commission
Federal Bldg., 28th Floor
915 Second Ave.
Seattle, WA 98174
(206) 442-4655

SECURITY DEPOSIT LIMITS BY STATE

State	Statutory Limit
Alabama	None
Alaska	Two month's rent
Arizona	One and one-half month's rent
Arkansas	Two month's rent
California	Two month's rent (unfurnished, no waterbed); two and one-half month's rent (unfurnished, with waterbed); three months rent (furnished, no waterbed); three and one-half month's rent (furnished, with waterbed)
Colorado	None
Connecticut	Two month's rent (tenant under 62 years of age); one month's rent (tenant 62 years of age or older)
Delaware	One month's rent on leases for one year or more; no limit for month-to-month rental agreements
D. C.	One month's rent
Florida	None
Georgia	None
Hawaii	One month's rent
Idaho	None
Illinois	None
Indiana	None
Iowa	Two month's rent
Kansas	One month's rent or one and one-half month's rent (unfurnished with pets, or furnished with no pets)
Kentucky	None
Louisiana	None
Maine	Two month's rent
Maryland	Whichever is greater: $50 or two month's rent
Massachusettes	Two month's rent
Michigan	One and one-half month's rent
Minnesota	None
Mississippi	None

Missouri	Two month's rent
Montana	None
Nebraska	One month's rent (no pets); one and one-quarter month's rent (with pets)
Nevada	Three month's rent
New Hampshire	One month's rent or $100, whichever is greatest.
New Jersey	One and one half-month's rent
New Mexico	One month's rent (for rental agreement less than one year); no limit for leases of one year or more
New York	None
North Carolina	One and one-half month's rent for month-to-month rental agreements; two months rent if term is longer than two months.
North Dakota	One month's rent
Ohio	None
Oklahoma	None
Oregon	None
Pennsylvania	Two month's rent for first year of renting; one month's rent during the second and subsequent years of renting
Rhode Island	One month's rent
South Carolina	None
South Dakota	One month's rent
Tennessee	None
Texas	None
Utah	None
Vermont	None
Virginia	Two month's rent
Washington	None
West Virginia	None
Wisconsin	None
Wyoming	None

Please note: these laws may have exceptions or exemptions, and are subject to change.

DEADLINES FOR RETURNING SECURITY DEPOSITS BY STATE

STATE	DEADLINE
Alabama	None
Alaska	14 days if the tenant gives proper notice to vacate , 30 if proper notice is not given.
Arizona	14 days
Arkansas	30 days
California	Three weeks
Colorado	30 days, unless longer period of time specified by lease agreement
Connecticut	Whichever is later: within 15 days of receipt of renter's forwarding address, or 30 days
Delaware	15 days
D.C.	45 days
Florida	15 to 45 days maximum if renter disputes deposit deductions
Georgia	30 days
Hawaii	14 days
Idaho	None
Illinois	30 days
Indiana	45 days
Iowa	30 days
Kansas	30 days
Kentucky	60 days
Louisiana	30 days
Maryland	45 days
Massachusetts	30 days
Michigan	30 days
Minnesota	21 days
Mississippi	45 days
Missouri	30 days
Montana	None
Nebraska	14 days
Nevada	30 days
New Hampshire	30 days
New Jersey	30 days

New Mexico	30 days
New York	Reasonable amount of time
North Carolina	30 days
North Dakota	30 days
Ohio	30 days
Oklahoma	30 days
Oregon	30 days
Pennsylvania	30 days
Rhode Island	20 days
South Carolina	20 days
South Dakota	Two weeks
Tennessee	None
Texas	30 days
Utah	Whichever is later: within 15 days of receipt of renter's forwarding address, or 30 days
Vermont	14 days
Virginia	30 days
Washington	14 days
West Virginia	None
Wisconsin	None
Wyoming	None

STATES THAT REQUIRE INTEREST ON DEPOSITS BE PAID TO THE RENTOR

Connecticut

District of Colombia

Florida*

Illinois

Iowa*

Maryland

Massachusetts

Minnesota

New Hampshire

New Jersey

New Mexico

New York

North Dakota

Ohio

Pennsylvania

Virginia

* Interest payments not required, but when made, certain conditions apply.

STATES THAT REQUIRE A SEPARATE ACCOUNT FOR SECURITY DEPOSITS

Alaska Deposit must be held in trust account or by escrow agent "wherever practicable."

Connecticut

Delaware

D.C.

Florida Landlord may post a bond rather than keeping a separate account.

Georgia Landlord may post a bond rather than keeping a separate account.

Iowa

Kentucky

Maine Deposit must be held in a special escrow account.

Maryland Deposit may not be held in an out of state bank.

Massachusetts Deposit may not be held in an out of state bank and must be in a special escrow account.

New Hampshire

New Jersey

New York

North Dakota

Oklahoma

Pennsylvania

Tennessee

Washington

DEPOSIT STATUTES THAT ALLOW NON-REFUNDABLE FEES BY STATE

In addition to having statutes which regulate the taking and maintenance of deposits, some states will also allow for certain non-refundable fees. The laws regarding a non-refundable fee, will vary greatly from state to state. The following states specifically allow such fees.

Arizona
Florida
Georgia
Nevada
New Jersey
North Carolina
Oregon
Utah
Washington

In some other states where there is no statute permitting non-refundable fees, there have been instances of state courts ruling that such fees are allowed. If non-refundable fees are of concern to you, further legal research would be encouraged.

STATE LAWS ON LATE FEES

Connecticut   No late fee may be charged until nine days after rent due. (Ex: Rent due on the 1st, no late fee charged till the 10th)

Delaware   In order for late fees to be charged there must be an office maintained in the county where the rental unit is located at which tenants can pay rent .

Maine   Late fees cannot exceed 4% of the amount due for 30 days. Landlord must notify tenants, in writing, of any late fee when you first sign a lease to move in.

Maryland   Late fees are not to exceed 5% of the rent due.

Massachusettes   **Rent must be 30 days late in order to charge a late fee**

Montana   Rent must be 30 days late before charging a late fee.

North Carolina   Rent must be five days late before charging a late fee, which is not to exceed 5% of the rental payment, or $15, whichever is higher.

Oregon   The late fee policy must be included in the lease, and no late fees may be assessed until 4 days after rent is due.

Tennessee   A late fee may not be charged until five days have passed. Fee is not to exceed 10% of the amount due.

NOTICE REQUIRED TO TERMINATE A MONTH-TO-MONTH TENANCY BY STATE

30 days is the notice required by the majority of states to terminate a month-to-month tenancy regardless of which party is terminating the agreement, tenant or landlord. There are, however, several states that have different statutes, they are as follows:

STATE	TENANT	LANDLORD
Alabama	10 days	10 days
Alaska	30 days	30 days
Colorado	10 days	10 days
Connecticut	30 days	30 days
Delaware	60 days	60 days
Florida	15 days	15 days
Georgia	30 days	60 days
Hawaii	28 days	45 days
Louisiana	10 days	10 days
Nevada	No statute	No statute
North Carolina	7 days	7 days
South Dakota	Mutual consent of parties	Same
Utah	No statute	No statute
Wisconsin	28 days	28 days
Wyoming	No statute	No statute

LAWS ON LANDLORD'S ACCESS TO RENTAL PROPERTY BY STATE

To enter a rental property, the landlord is legally required to give the tenant the following notice even in states with "no specific statute," "reasonable notice" should be given:

STATE	NOTICE REQUIRED
Alabama	No specific statute
Alaska	24 Hours
Arizona	48 Hours
Arkansas	No specific statute
California	24 Hours
Colorado	No specific statute
Conn.	Reasonable notice
Delaware	48 Hours
D. C.	No specific statute
Florida	12 Hours
Georgia	No specific statute
Hawaii	48 Hours
Idaho	No specific statute
Illinois	No specific statute
Indiana	No specific statute
Iowa	24 Hours
Kansas	Reasonable notice
Kentucky	48 Hours
Louisiana	No specific statute
Maine	24 Hours
Maryland	No specific statute
Mass.	No specific statute
Michigan	No specific statute
Minnesota	No specific statute
Mississippi	No specific statute
Missouri	No specific statute
Montana	24 Hours
Nebraska	24 Hours
Nevada	24 Hours
New Hampshire	No specific statute
New Jersey	No specific statute
New Mexico	No specific statute

New York	No specific statute
North Carolina	No specific statute
North Dakota	Reasonable notice
Ohio	24 Hours
Oklahoma	24 Hours
Oregon	24 Hours
Pennsylvania	No specific statute
Rhode Island	48 Hours
South Carolina	24 Hours
South Dakota	No specific statute
Tennessee	No specific statute
Texas	No specific statute
Utah	No specific statute
Vermont	48 Hours
Virginia	Reasonable notice
Washington	48 Hours
West Virginia	No specific statute
Wisconsin	Reasonable notice
Wyoming	No specific statute

Please note: these laws may have exceptions or exemptions, and are subject to change. States that do not require landlords to give a fixed amount of notice before entering property may still limit landlords' access to rental properties. Consult a local attorney or a housing agency in your area for more information.

STATES THAT ALLOW TENANTS TO REPAIR AND DEDUCT

If the landlord has failed to make requested repairs within a reasonable time, the following states allow tenants to subtract the cost of those repairs from the rent owed.

Alaska
Arizona
California
Connecticut
Delaware
Hawaii
Iowa
Kentucky
Louisiana
Maine
Massachusetts
Minnesota
Mississippi
Montana
Nebraska
Nevada
New Mexico
New York
Oklahoma
Oregon
Rhode Island
South Carolina
South Dakota
Tennessee
Texas
Vermont
Virginia
Washington

Rules vary from state to state. Check your local laws before using a repair and deduct remedy.

STATES THAT ALLOW RENT WITHHOLDING

The following states allow tenants to withhold rent until their landlords remedy conditions that have made the property unfit for habitation.

Alaska
Arizona
California
Connecticut
Florida
Georgia
Hawaii
Illinois
Iowa
Kansas
Kentucky
Maine
Maryland
Minnesota
Missouri
Montana
Nebraska
Nevada
New Hampshire
New Mexico
New York
Ohio
Oregon
Pennsylvania
Rhode Island
South Carolina
South Dakota
Vermont
Virginia
Washington

Rules vary from state to state. Check your local laws before withholding any rent.

Disclaimer

The purpose of this publication is to give you general information. It is in no way designed or intended to provide legal advice or specific recommendations. Laws and rules change frequently. The accuracy of laws or recommendation can not be guaranteed. Please consult an attorney and/or accountant before acting upon any of this general information.

Special Offer

You can join the National Association for Renters' Rights to get help and advice about any landlord problems or questions that you might have.

The National Association for Renters' Rights is the only National group dedicated to you and protecting your rights as a renter. You will receive:

- The Association's problem resolution service. Any question or problem you have will be answered by the Association

- The Association will help you and work on your behalf if you have a problem with your landlord

- Special local resources that you can use for free in your area to help you as a renter

- Hundreds of dollars worth of money saving bonuses

- An ironclad unconditional money back guarantee.

You have nothing to risk. Normally, the membership costs $59.95. For a limited time if you call 1-800-RENT588 or 1-800-736-8588 you will get all the benefits of members for only $39.95. Please mention that you already own the *Renter's Rights Handbook* and tell the operator where you bought it.

Call Now.

1-800-RENT588

About the Author

Robert D. Shemin holds both a Law and MBA degree from Emory University. He is a landlord who believes that all renters should be treated like valued customers.

Shemin has lectured to thousands of landlords around the country and has helped many renters become homeowners and real estate investors through his first book— *Honest Profits: Your Hands-On Guide to Successful Real Estate Investing.* He is also known for creating a program known as The National Landlord Challenge which helps homeless families live in a house for a year for free so that they then have enough of a downpayment to become homeowners. Shemin has appeared on many national T.V. talk shows and speaks all over the country about Renters' Rights. You can contact him at:

Robert Shemin
P.O. Box 128186
Nashville, TN 37212-8186

Homepage Website: www.Rent.588.com

You can order *Honest Profits: Your Hands-On Guide to Real Estate Investing* by calling 1-800-RENT588. To order more copies of *The Renter's Rights Handbook* for your friends, neighbors or family—call 1-800-RENT588.